Abstract Reverse Coloring Book for Anxiety Relief

Amina Kan

"Abstract art is a way of giving a voice to the soul"
-Nancy Hellebrand

Welcome to the captivating world of "Abstract Reverse Coloring Book for anxiety relief." Prepare to embark on a whimsical journey through a realm where vibrant colors and abstract forms intertwine to create breathtaking works of art. In this book, we invite you to explore the enchanting realm of abstract painting, where imagination knows no bounds.

Within the pages of this extraordinary book, you will enter a realm where artistic expression takes on a delightful twist. Delicate lines and imaginative patterns dance across mesmerizing backgrounds, forming a symphony of abstract masterpieces that challenge traditional representations. Brace yourself for a transformative experience as you unleash your creativity upon each page, bringing to life a fusion of colors and shapes that celebrate the boundless realm of artistic imagination.

Prepare to be captivated by a tapestry of whimsy and abstraction, where the ordinary becomes extraordinary. As you journey deeper into this world, you'll find yourself immersed in a vibrant landscape that invites you to explore the limitless possibilities of abstract art. Each stroke of your drawing instrument will unveil a new layer of magic, revealing the hidden beauty and unexpected connections that lie within the abstract realms of artistry.

Embrace the adventure that awaits you in "Abstract Reverse Coloring Book for anxiety relief." Let your artistic spirit soar as you explore the uncharted territories of whimsical abstraction. Immerse yourself in a realm where colors and forms intertwine, allowing your imagination to run wild and creating a visual symphony that celebrates the beauty of abstract art. Get ready to embark on an unforgettable journey where creativity knows no boundaries and every page holds a delightful surprise.

Elkran :)

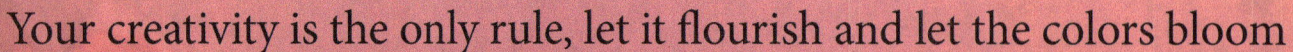

Your creativity is the only rule, let it flourish and let the colors bloom

Feel free to unleash your artistic spirit using any pen, any size, and any color that resonates with you. Whether you prefer bold strokes or delicate lines, this book encourages you to explore a vast array of artistic expressions. Embrace the freedom to create shapes beyond the confines of tradition. From squares to circles, from intricate details to minimalistic designs, let your imagination

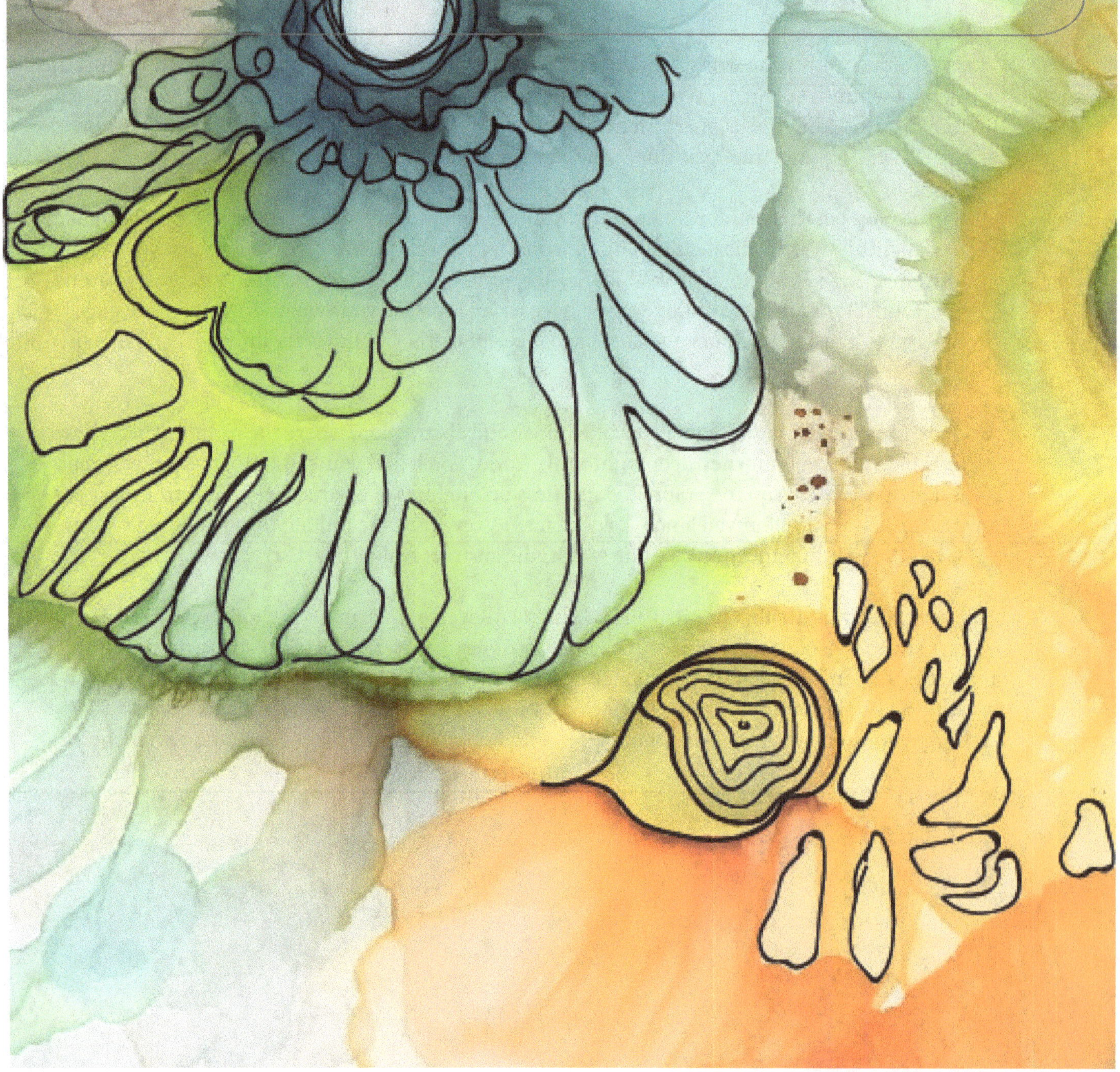

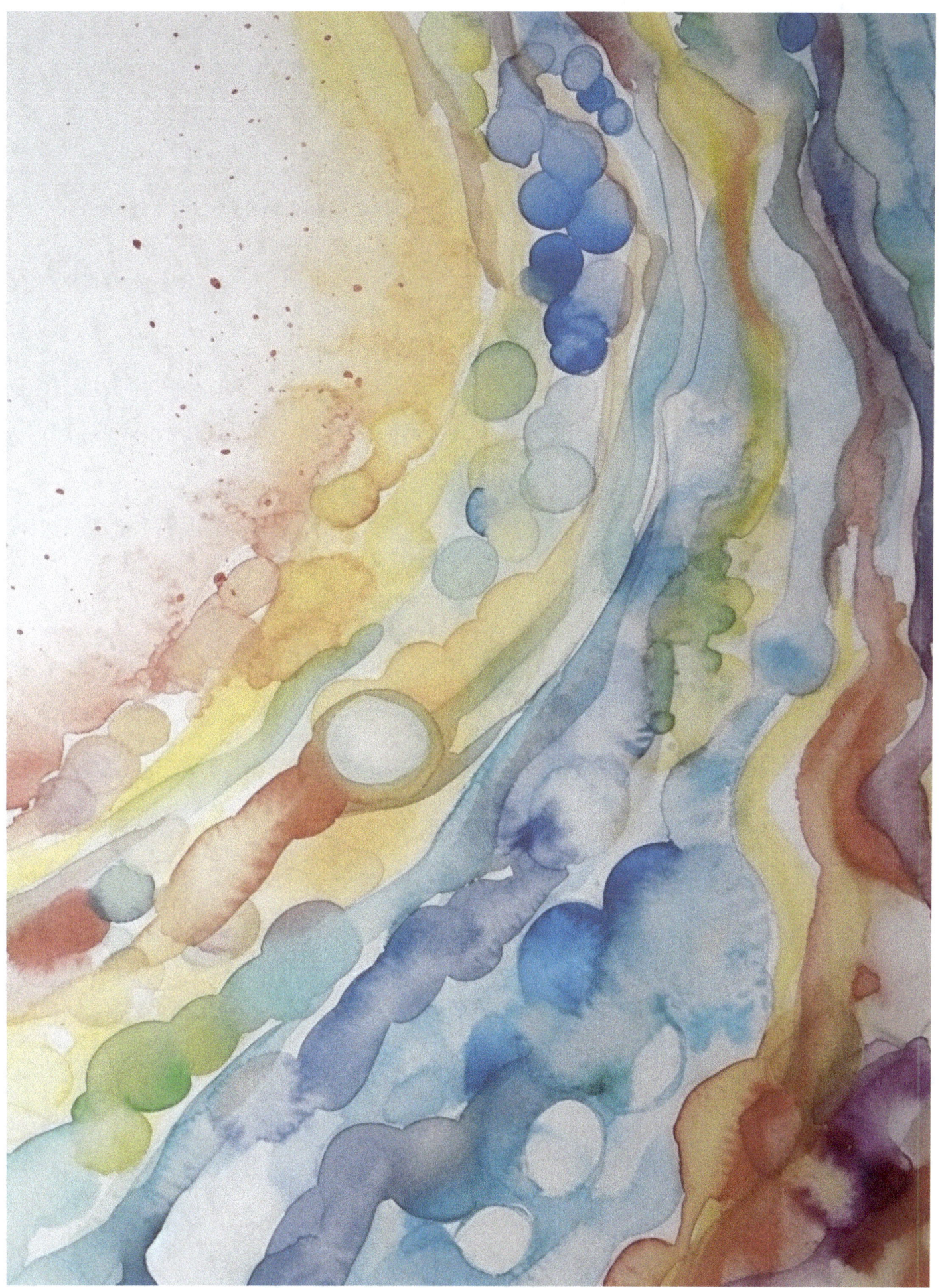

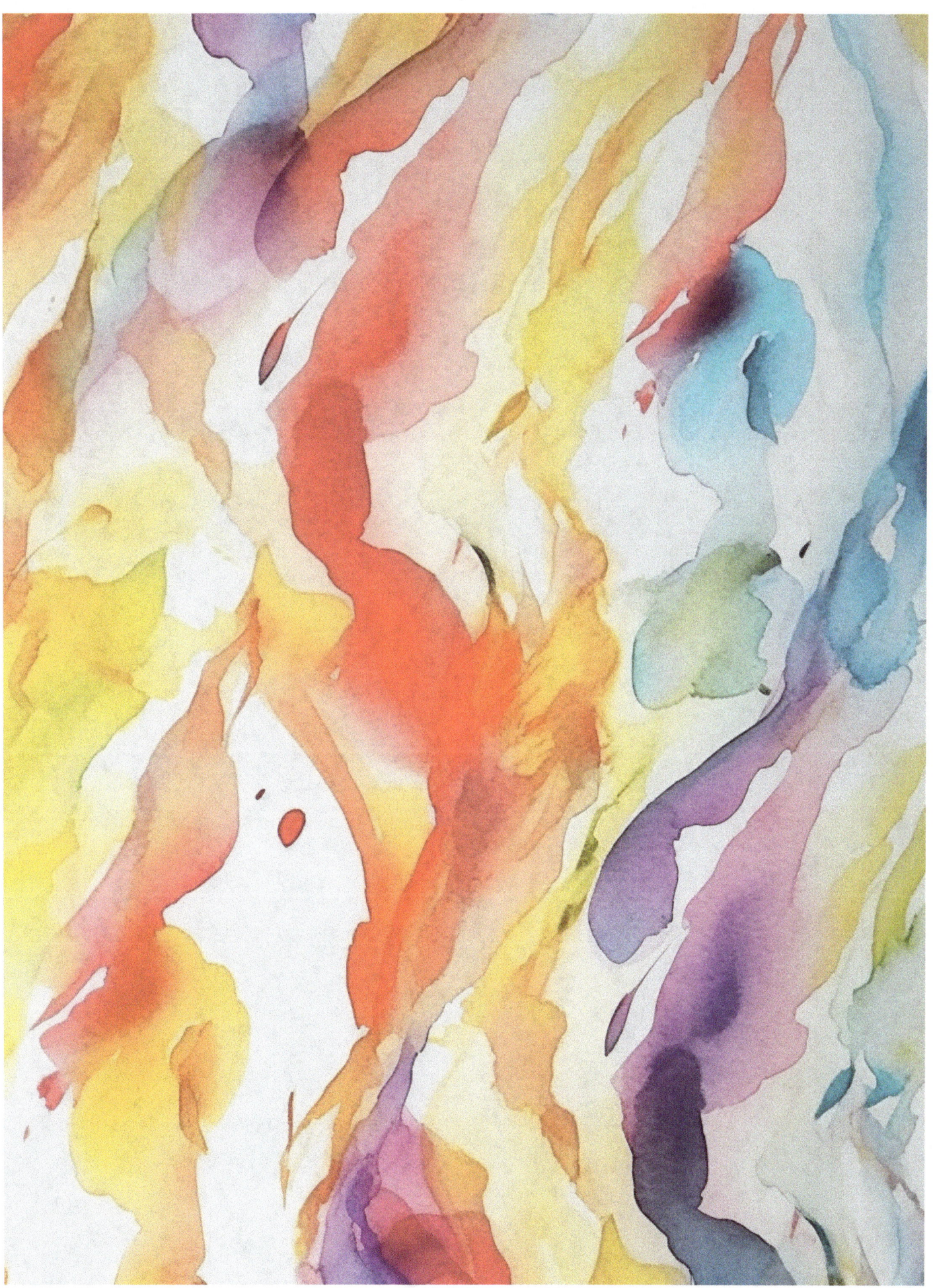

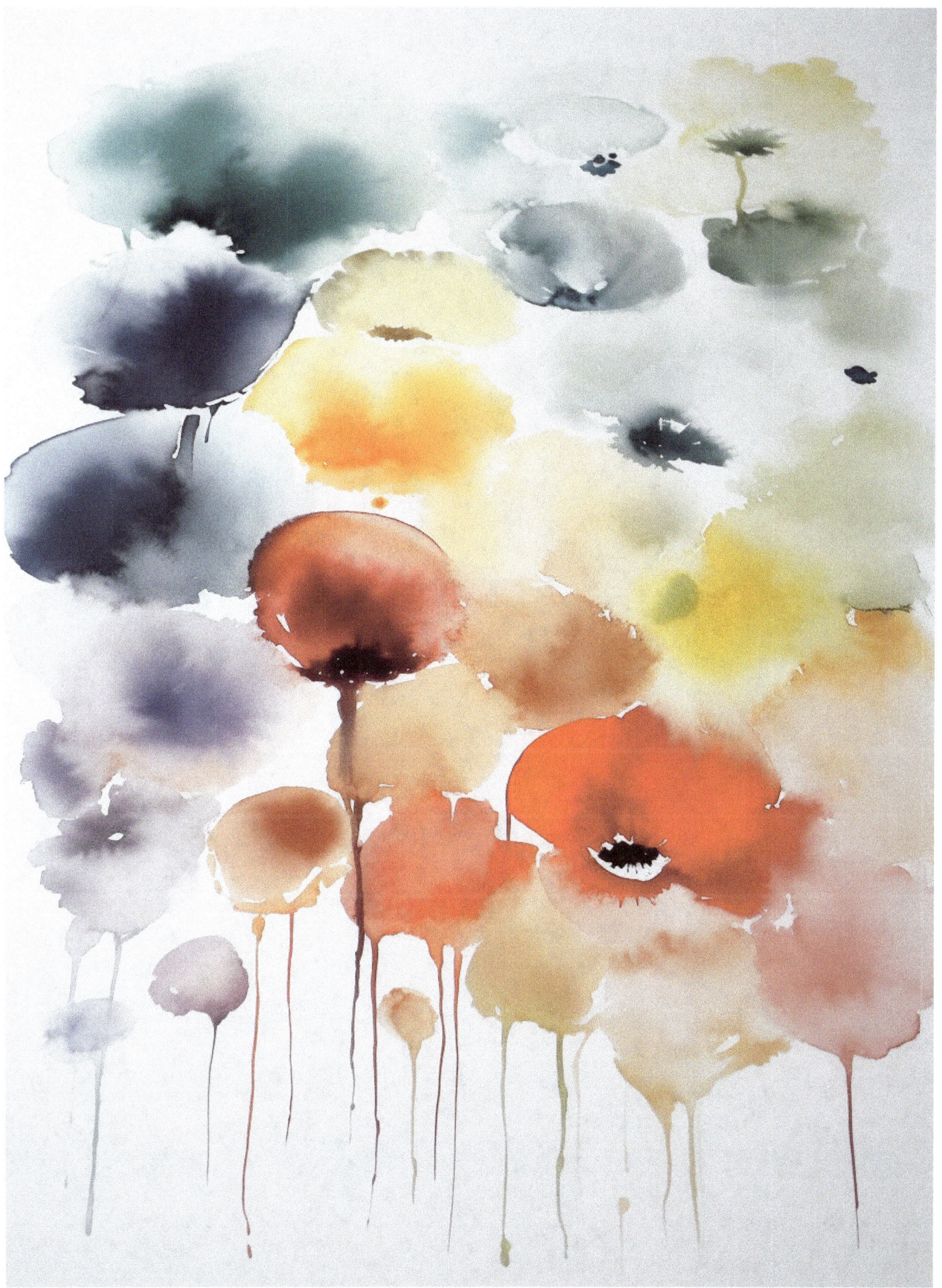

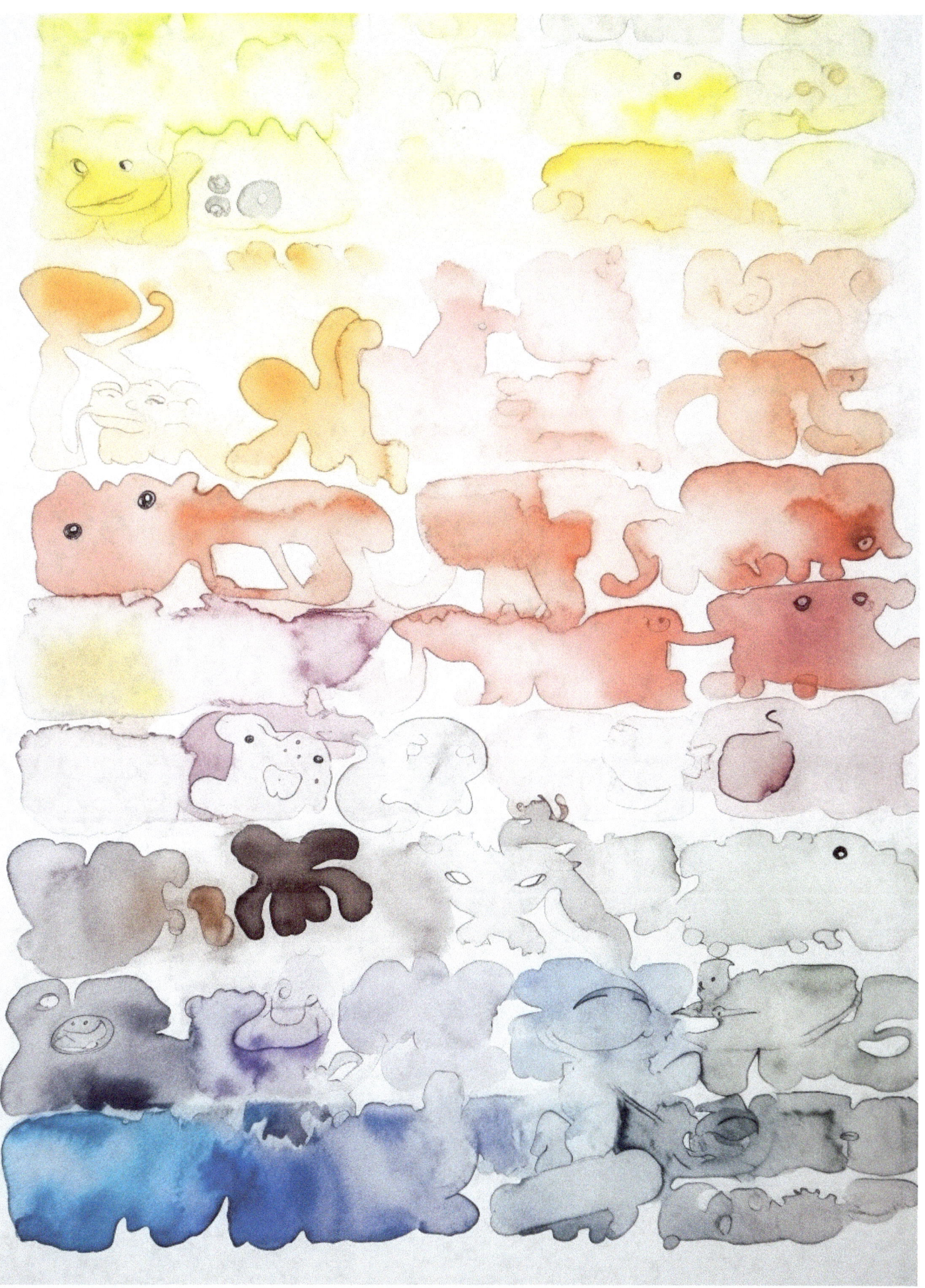

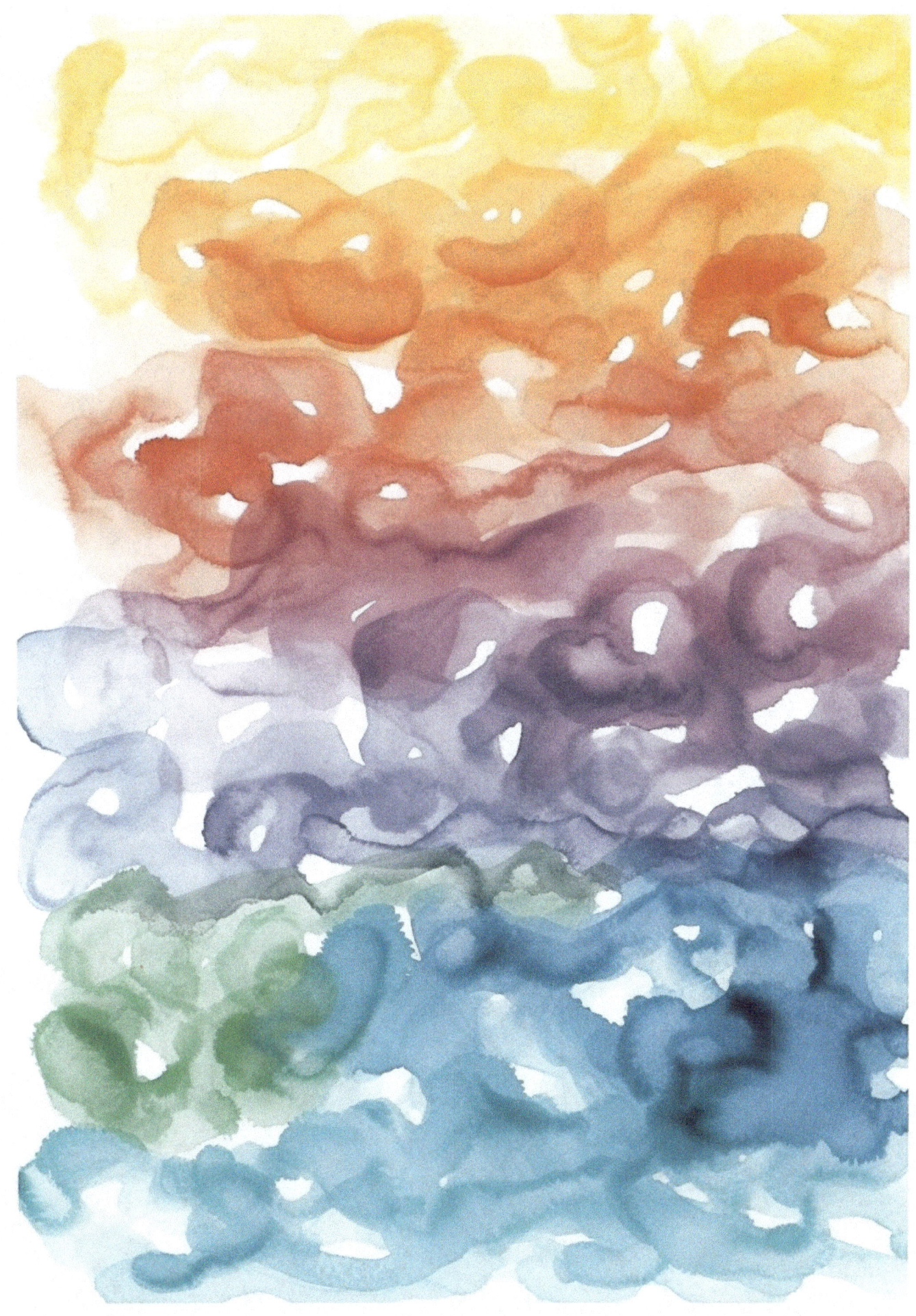

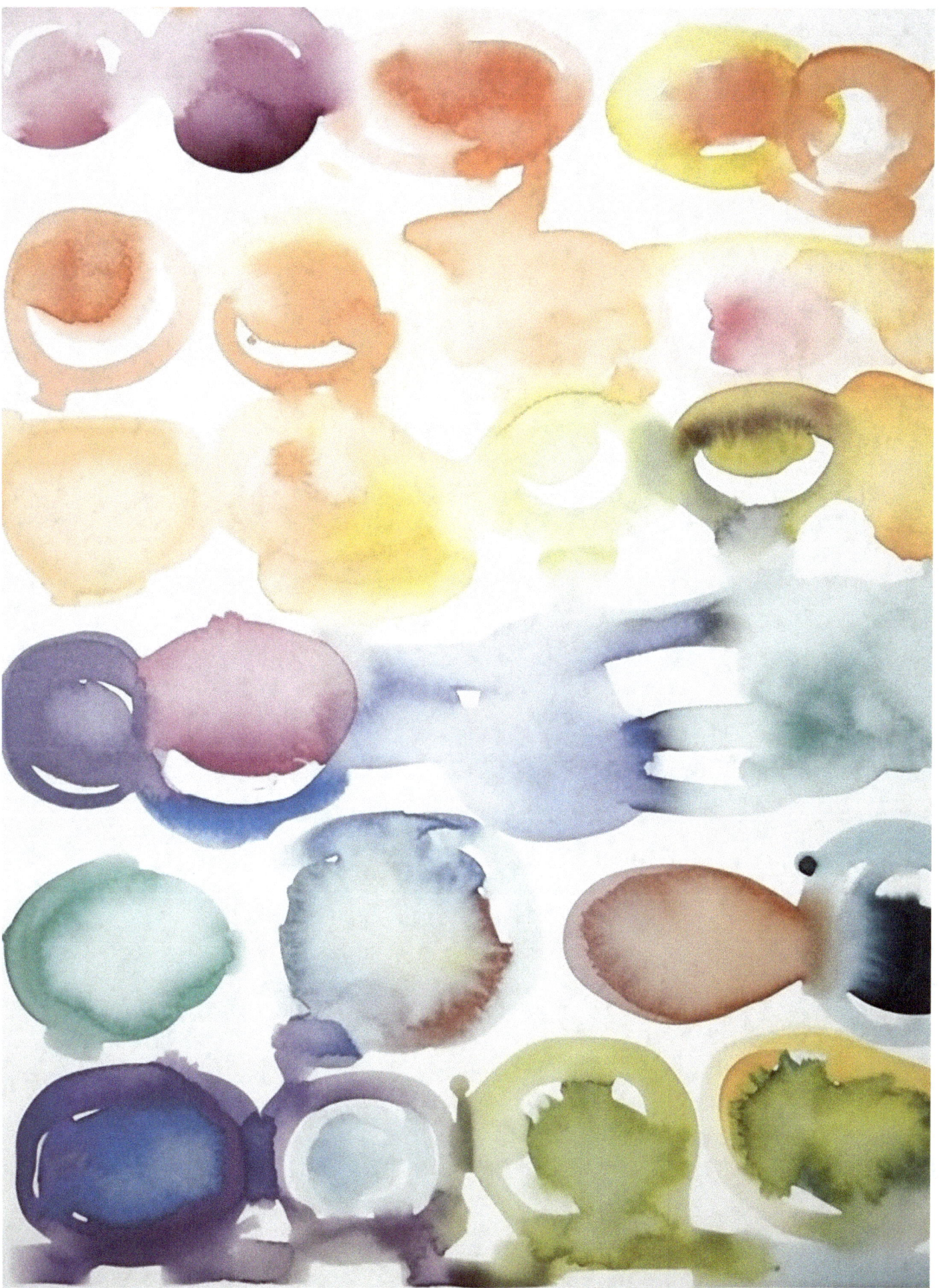

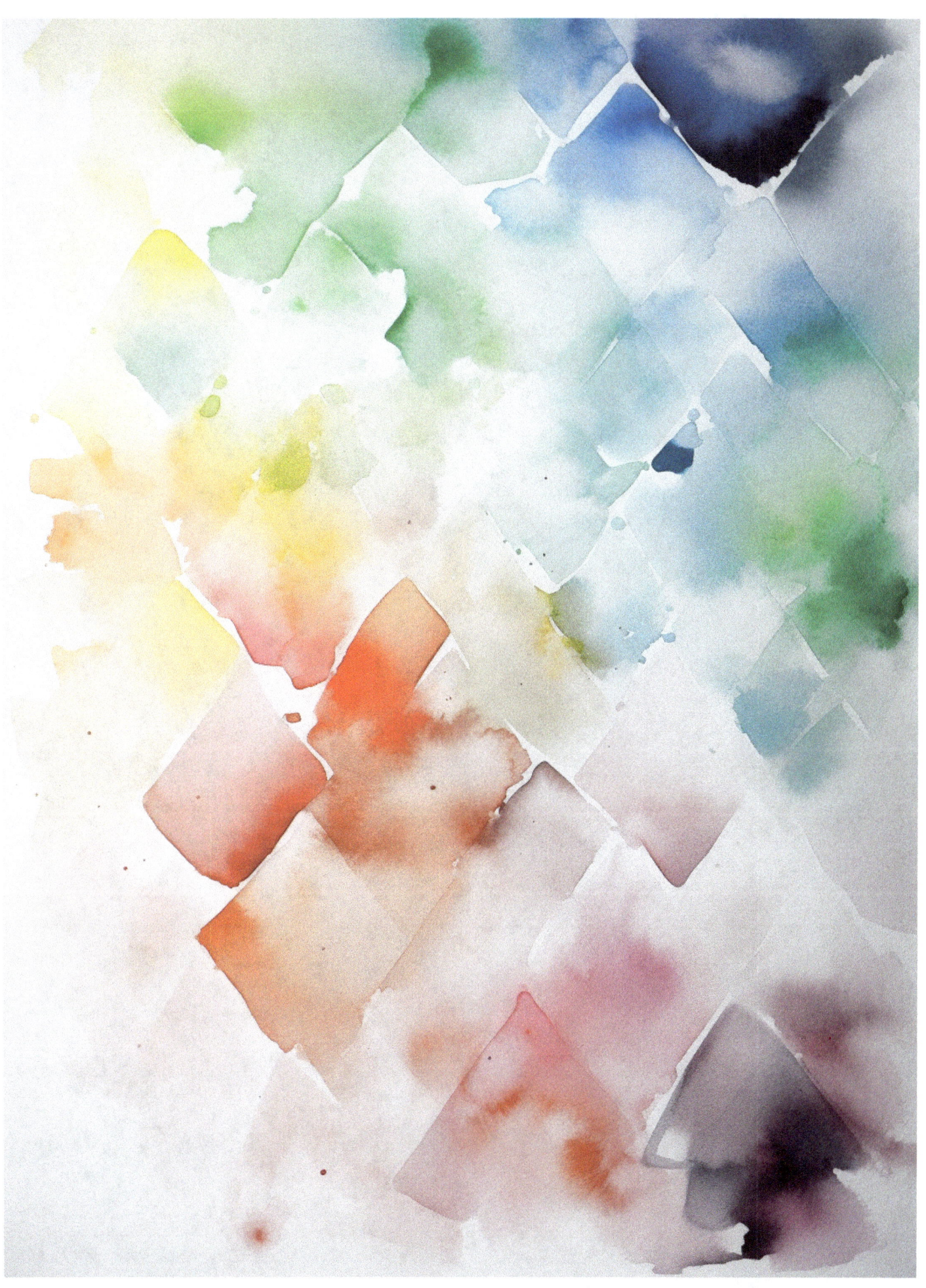

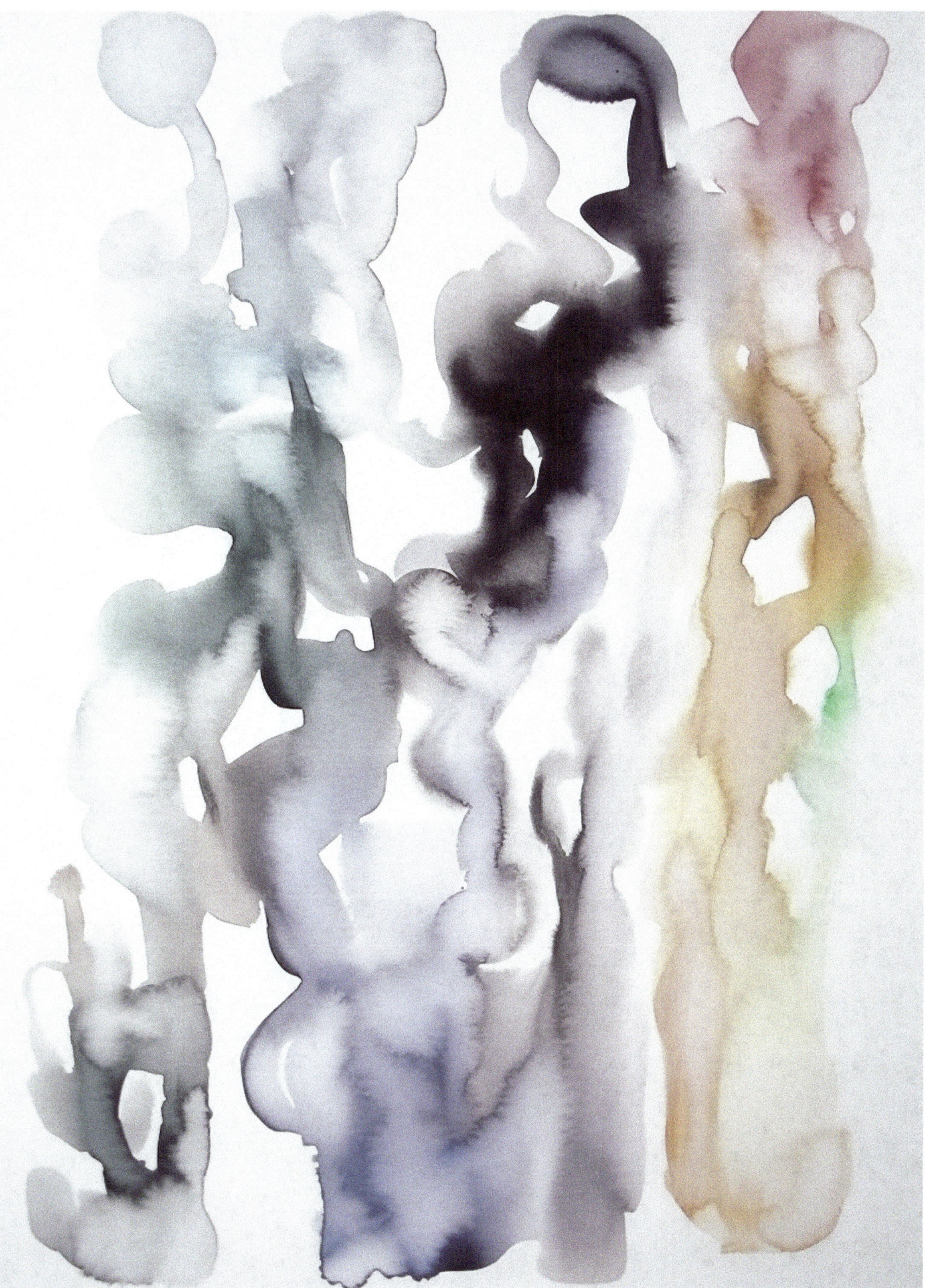

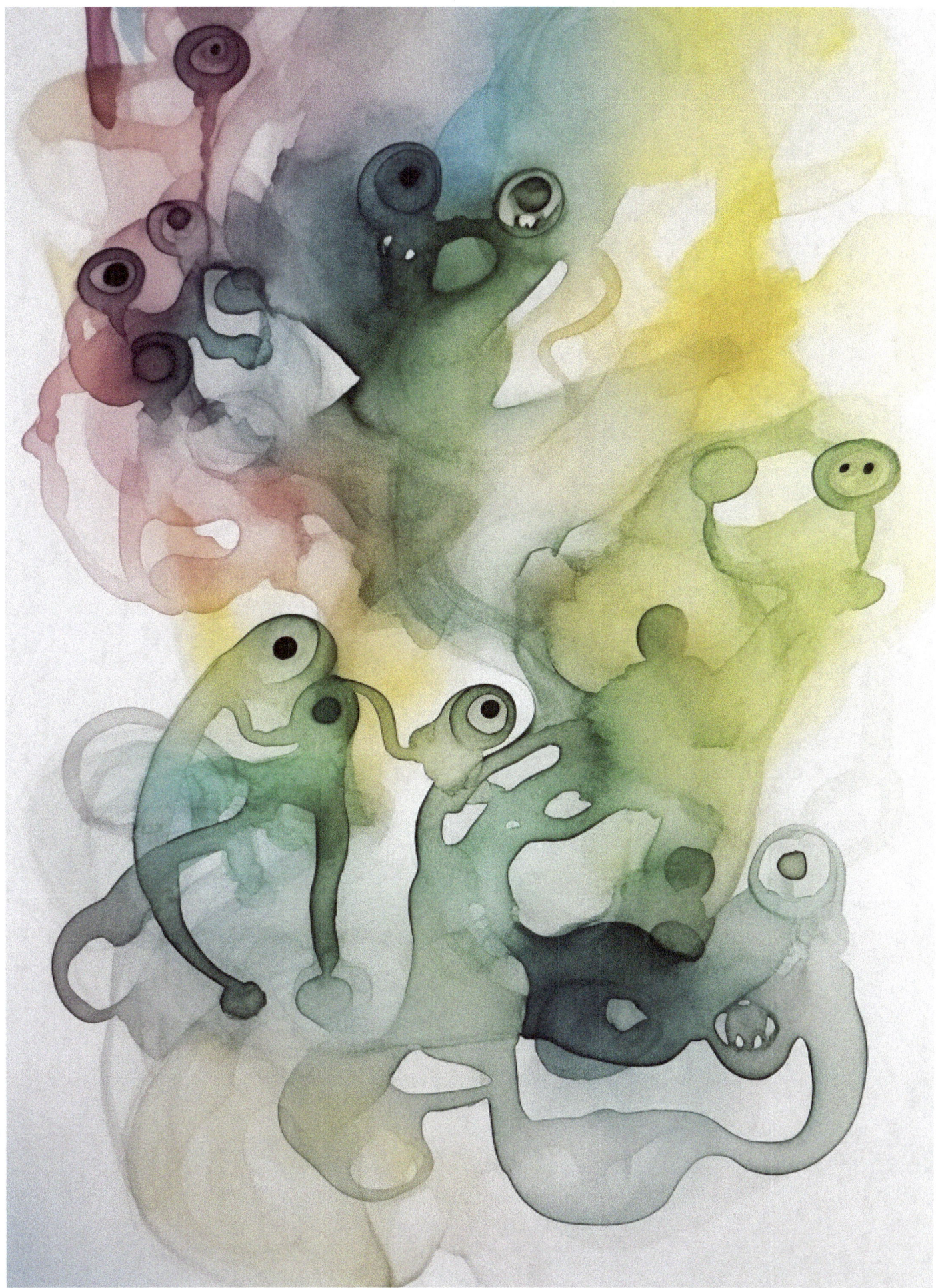

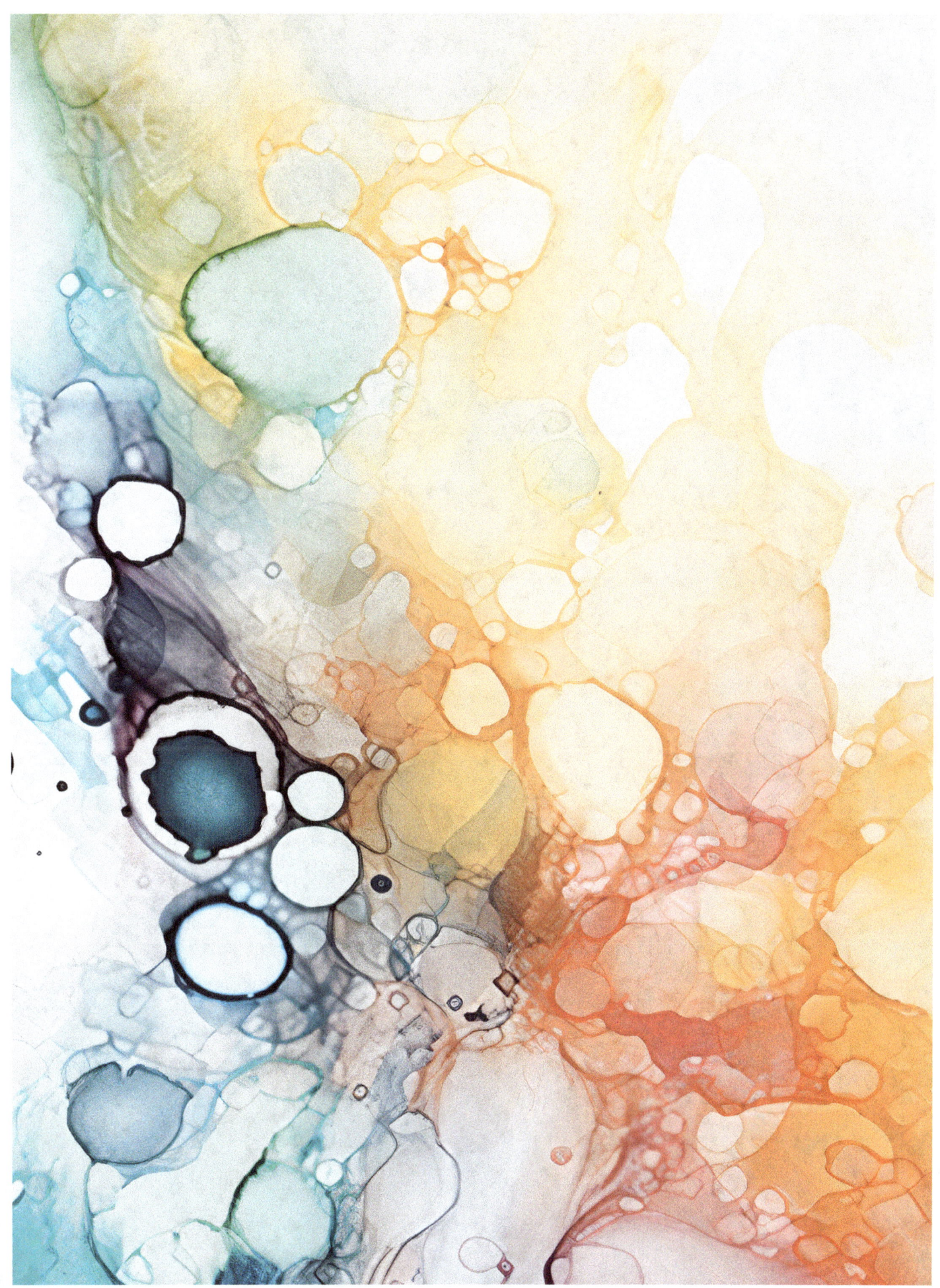

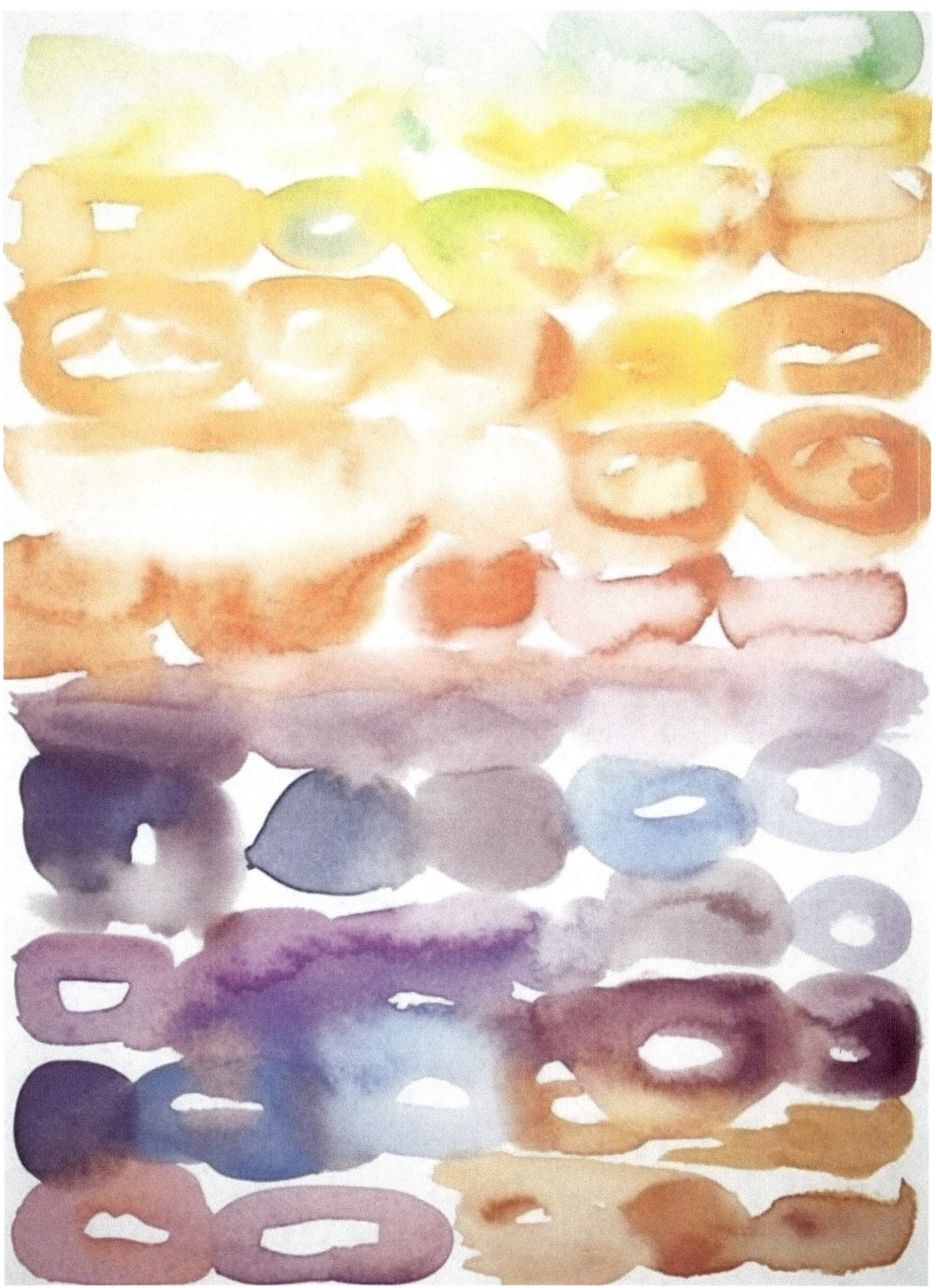

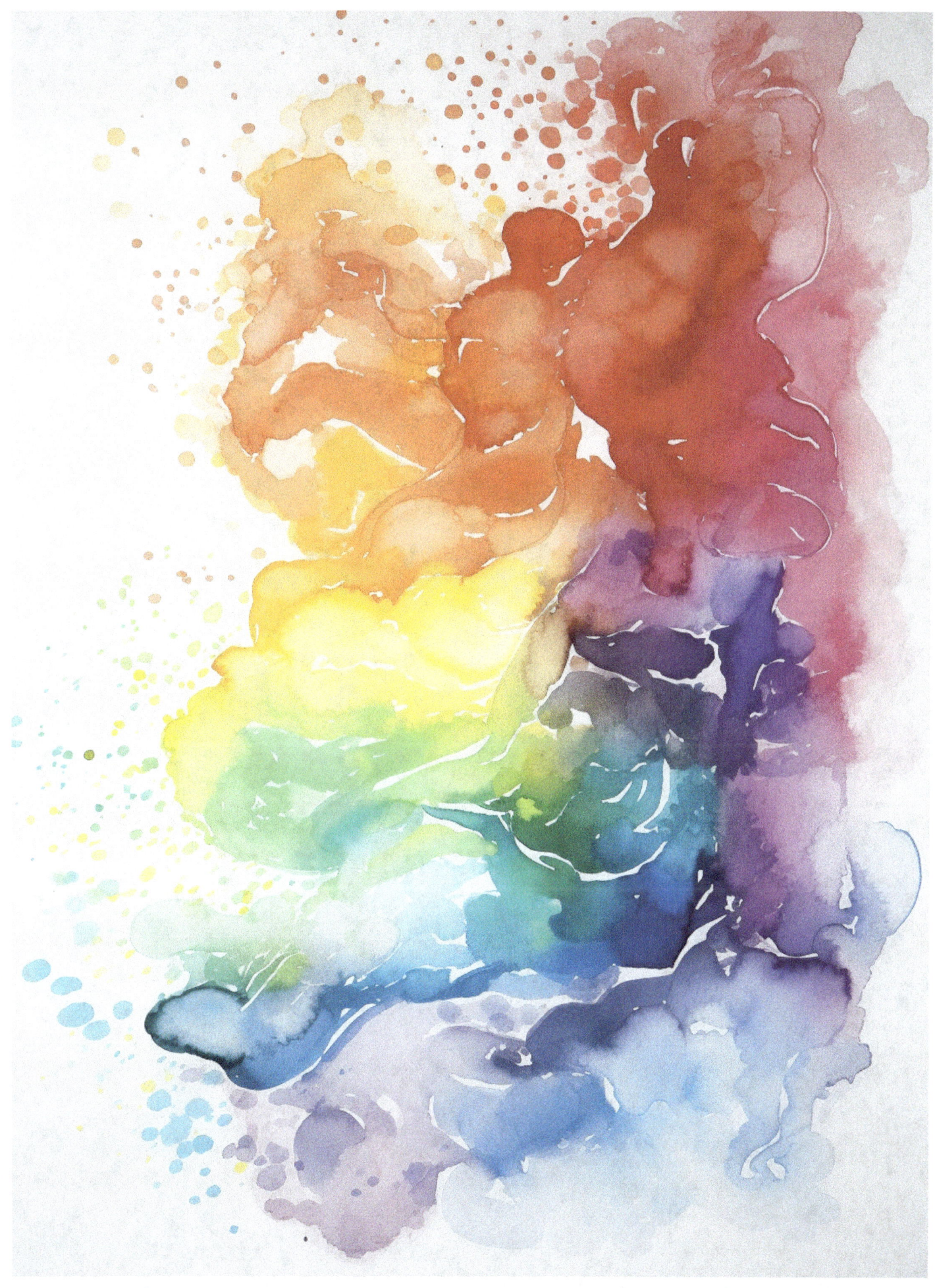

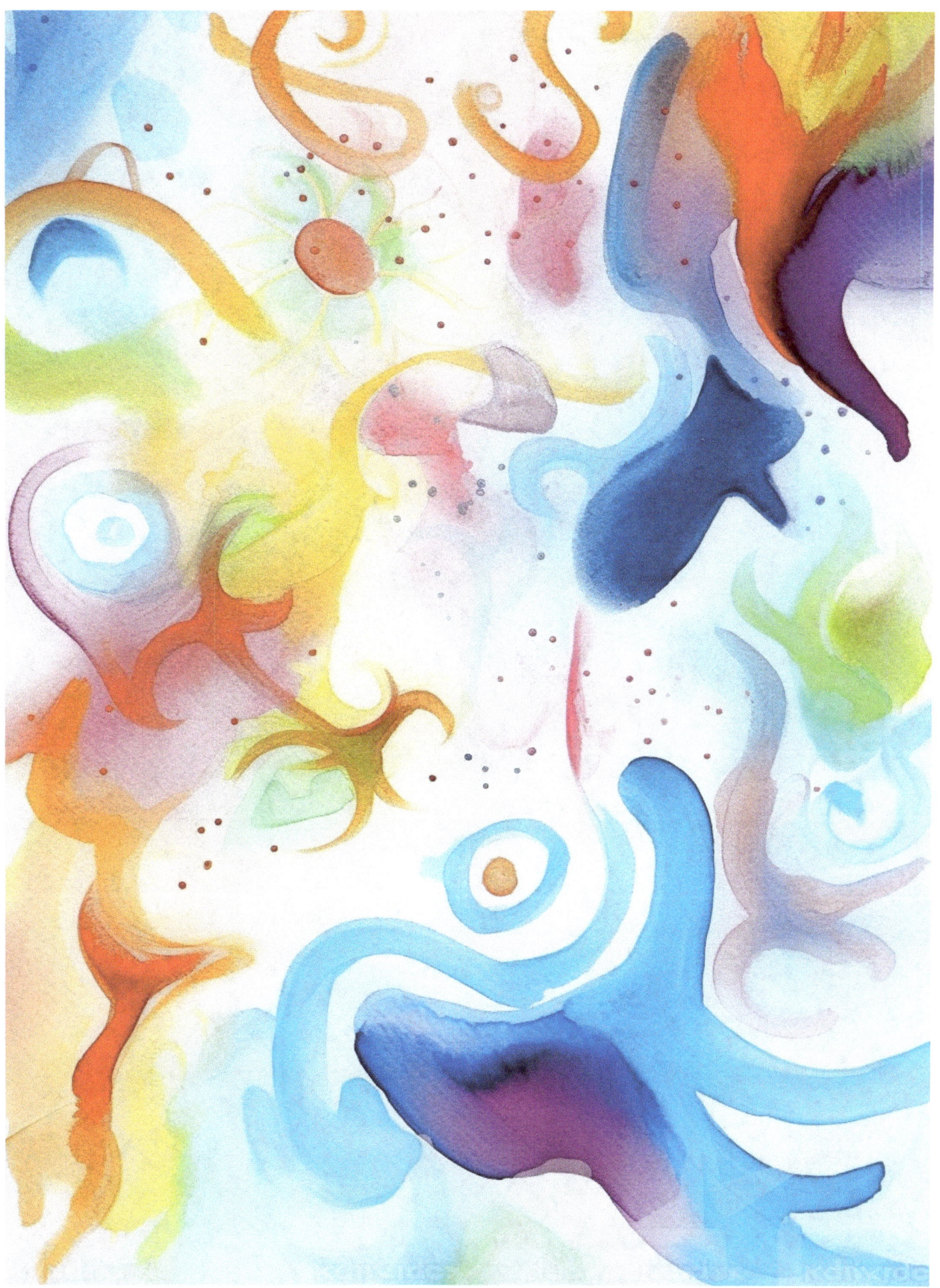

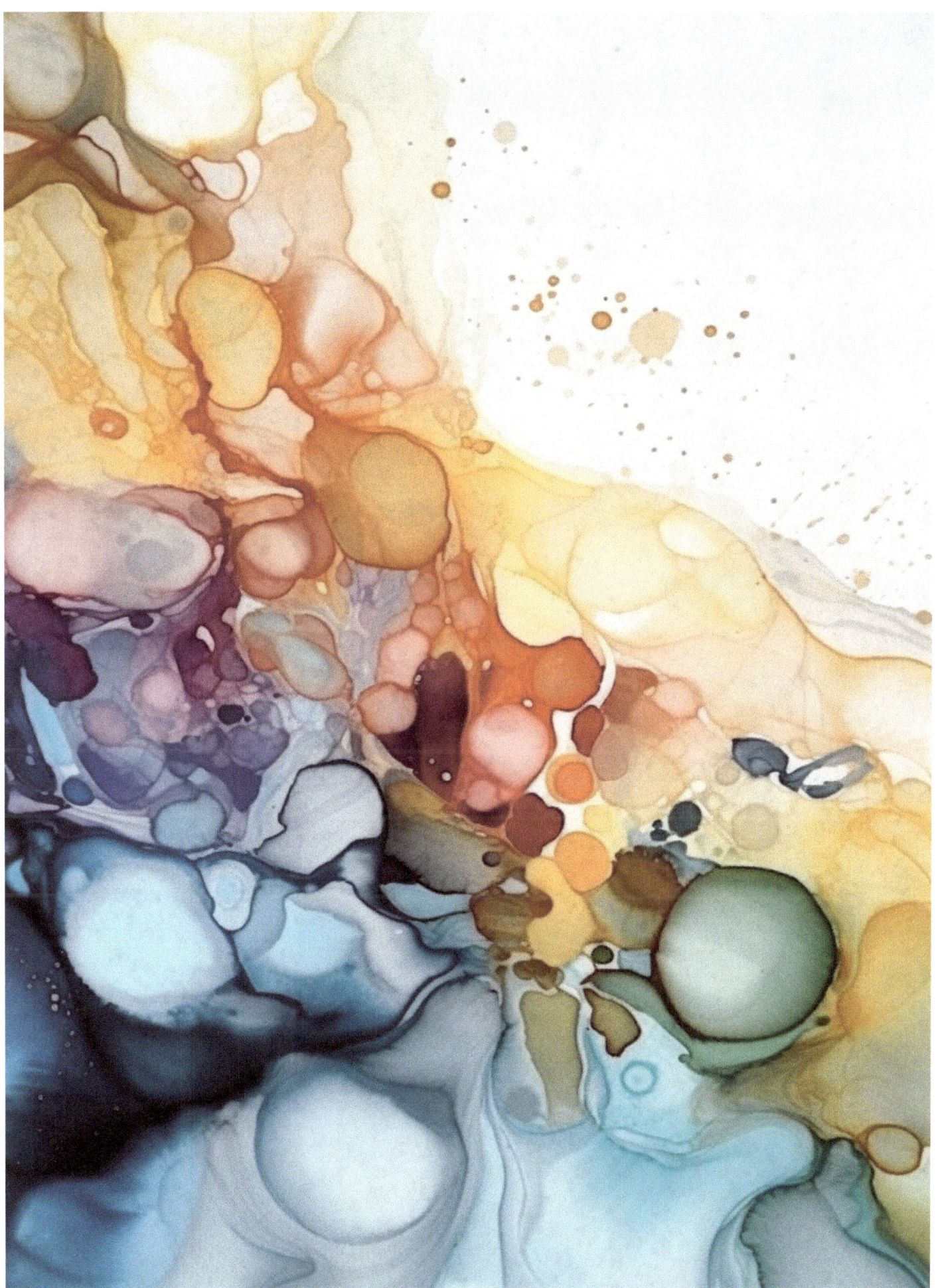

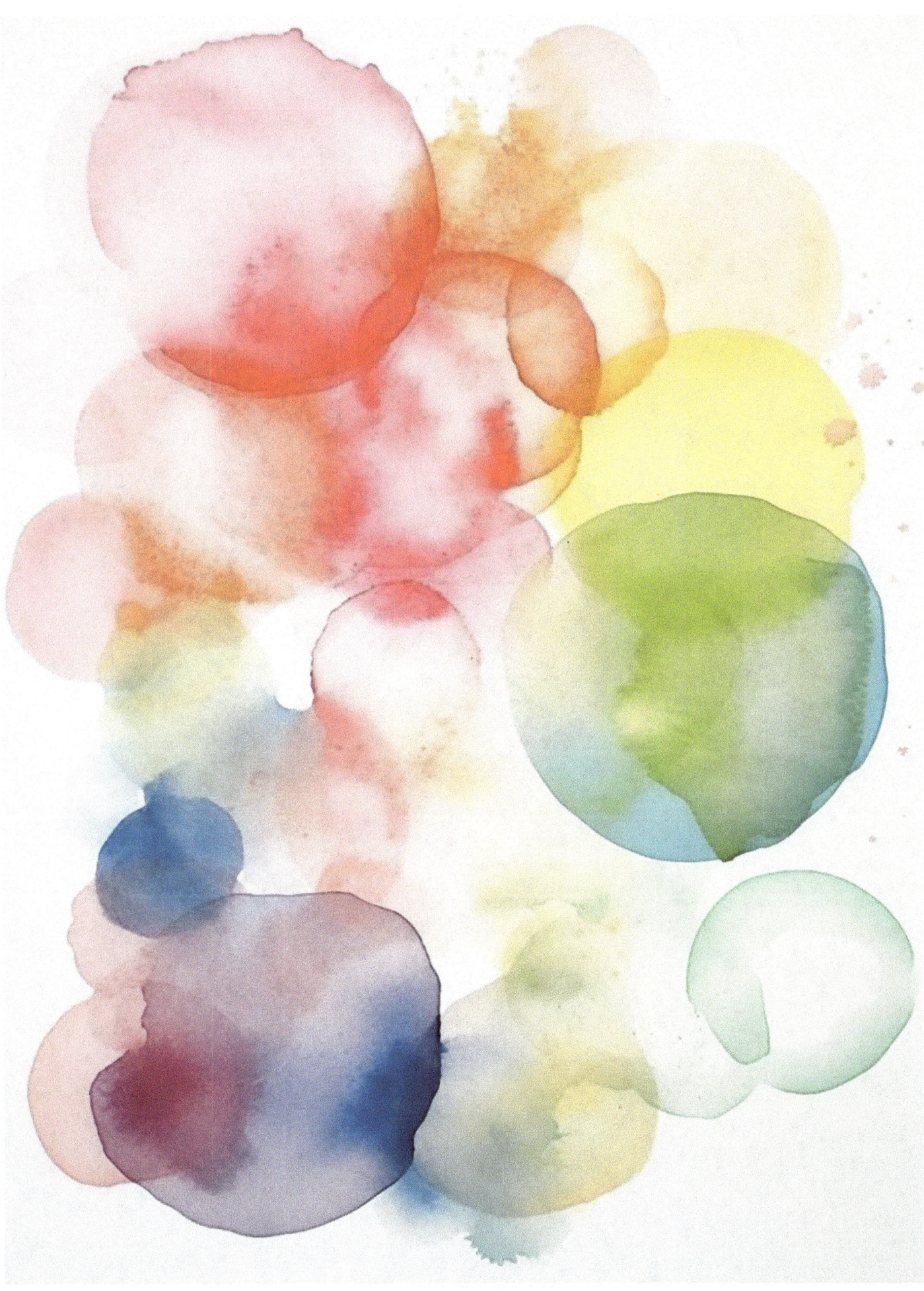

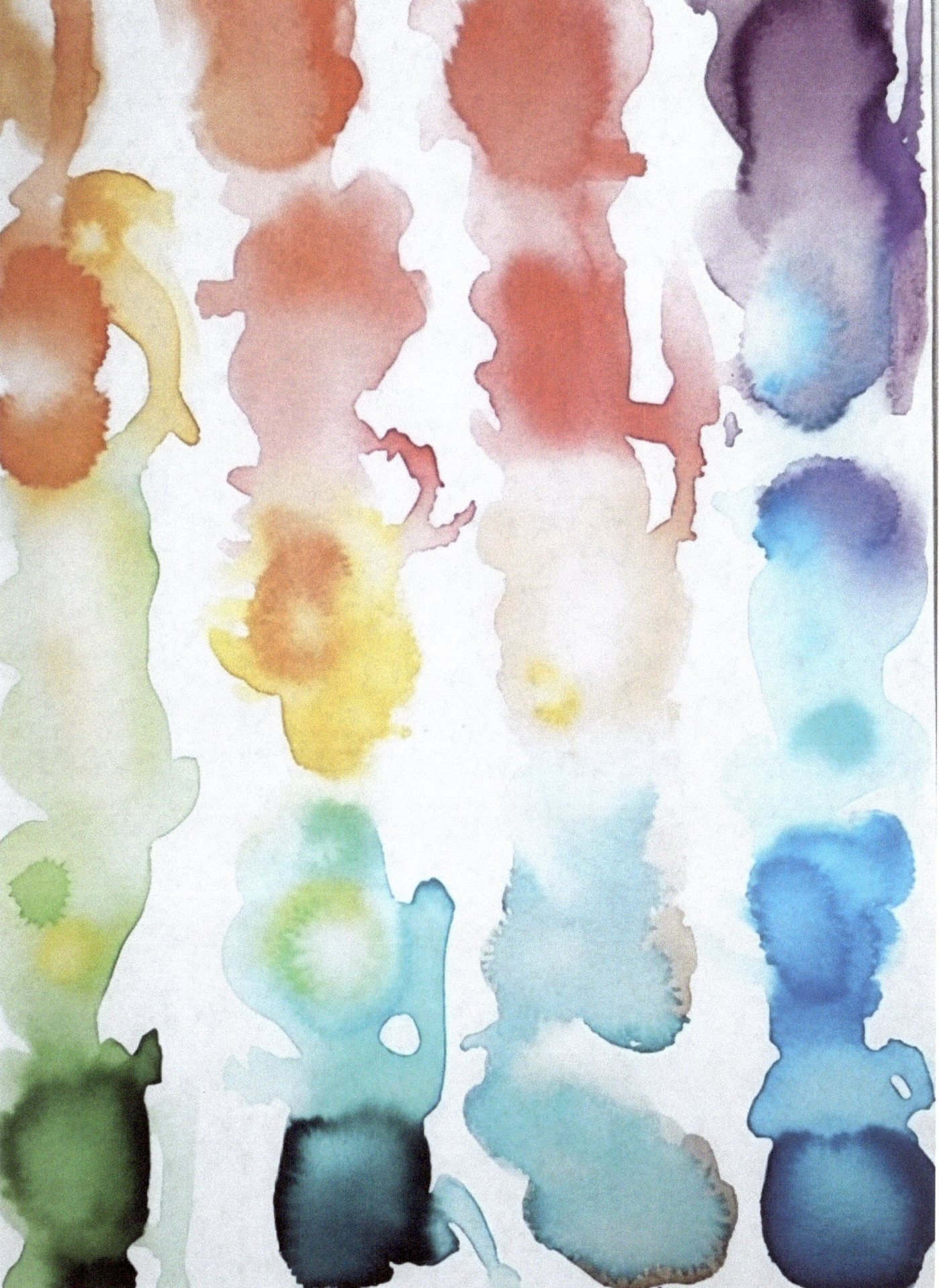

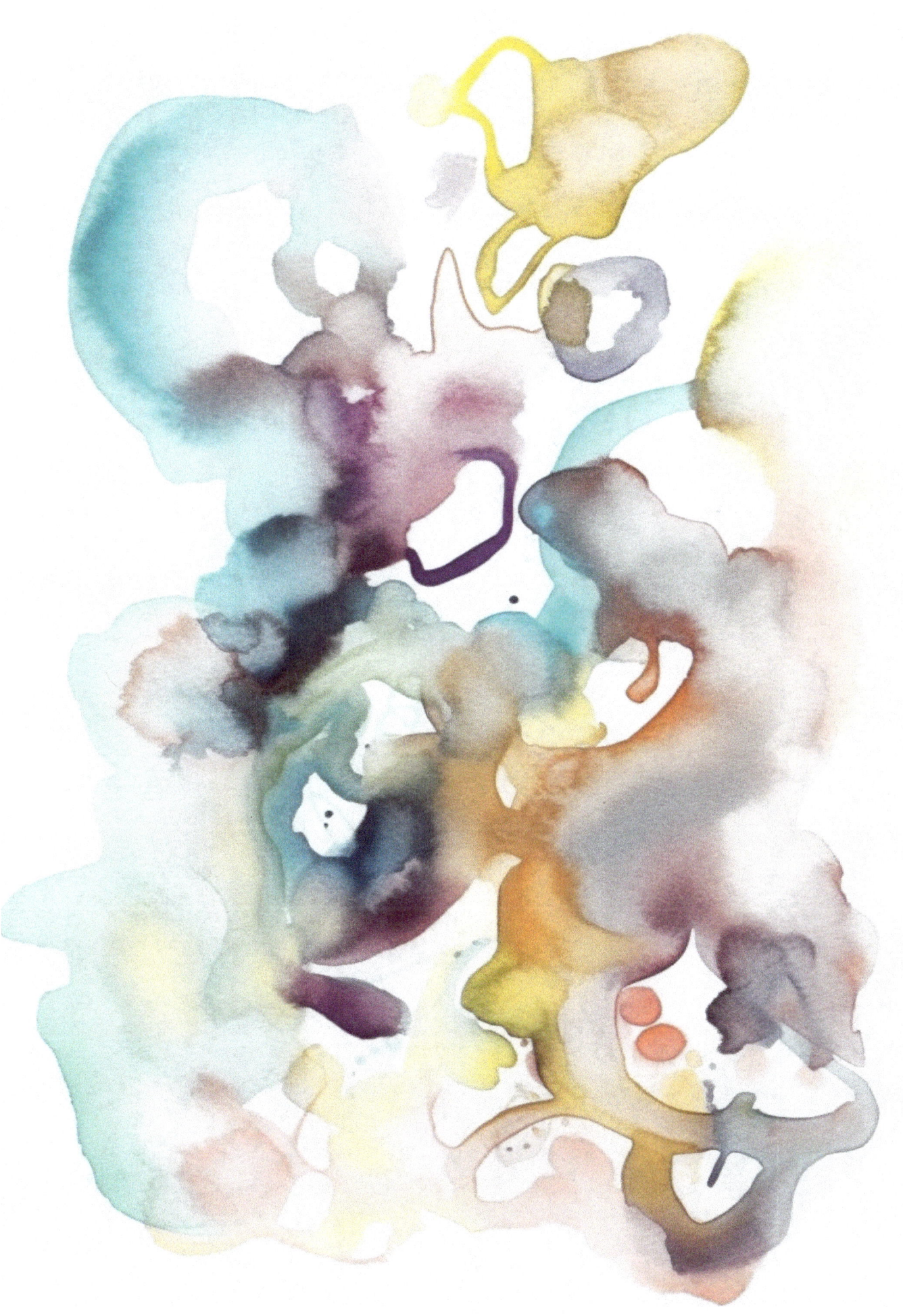

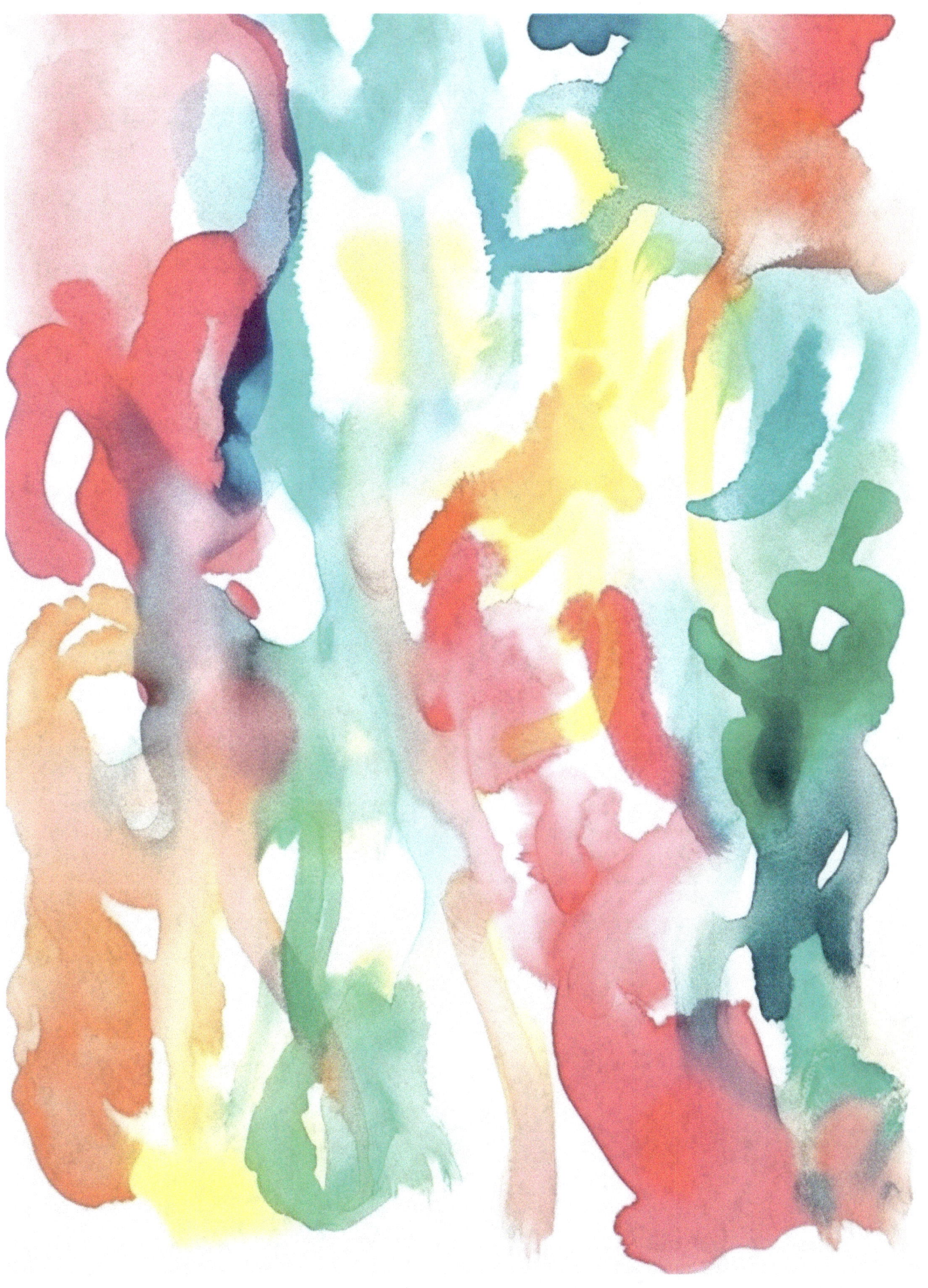

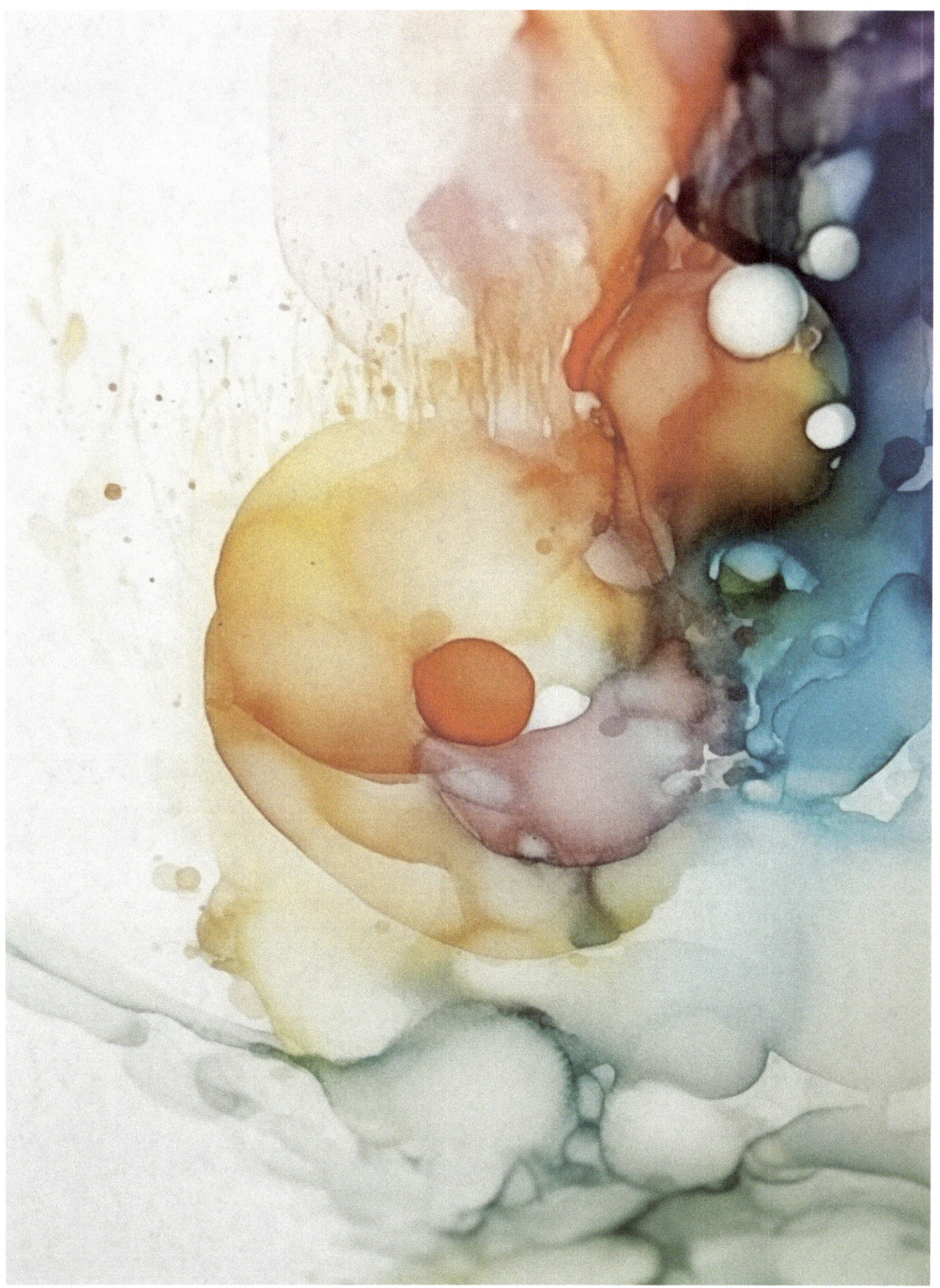

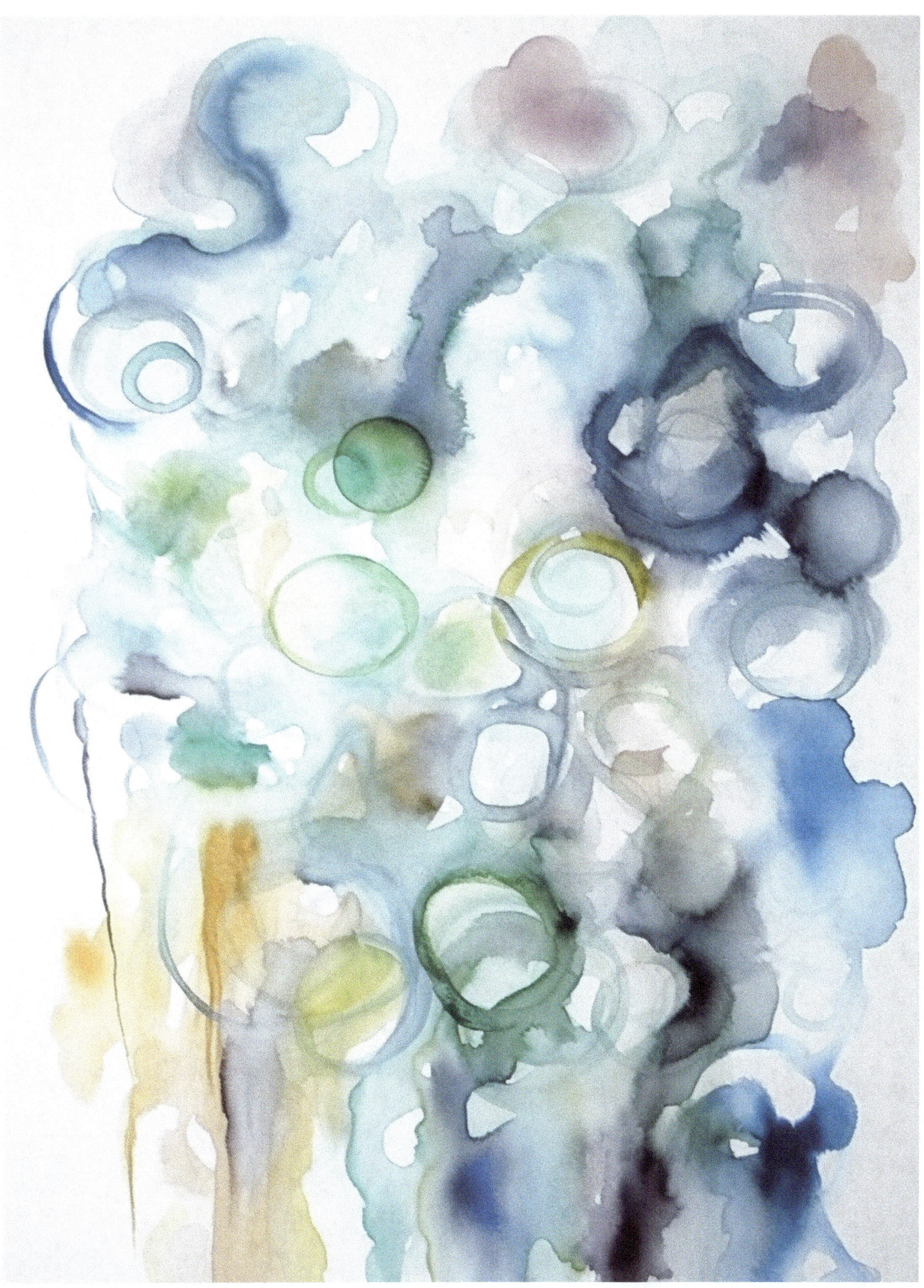

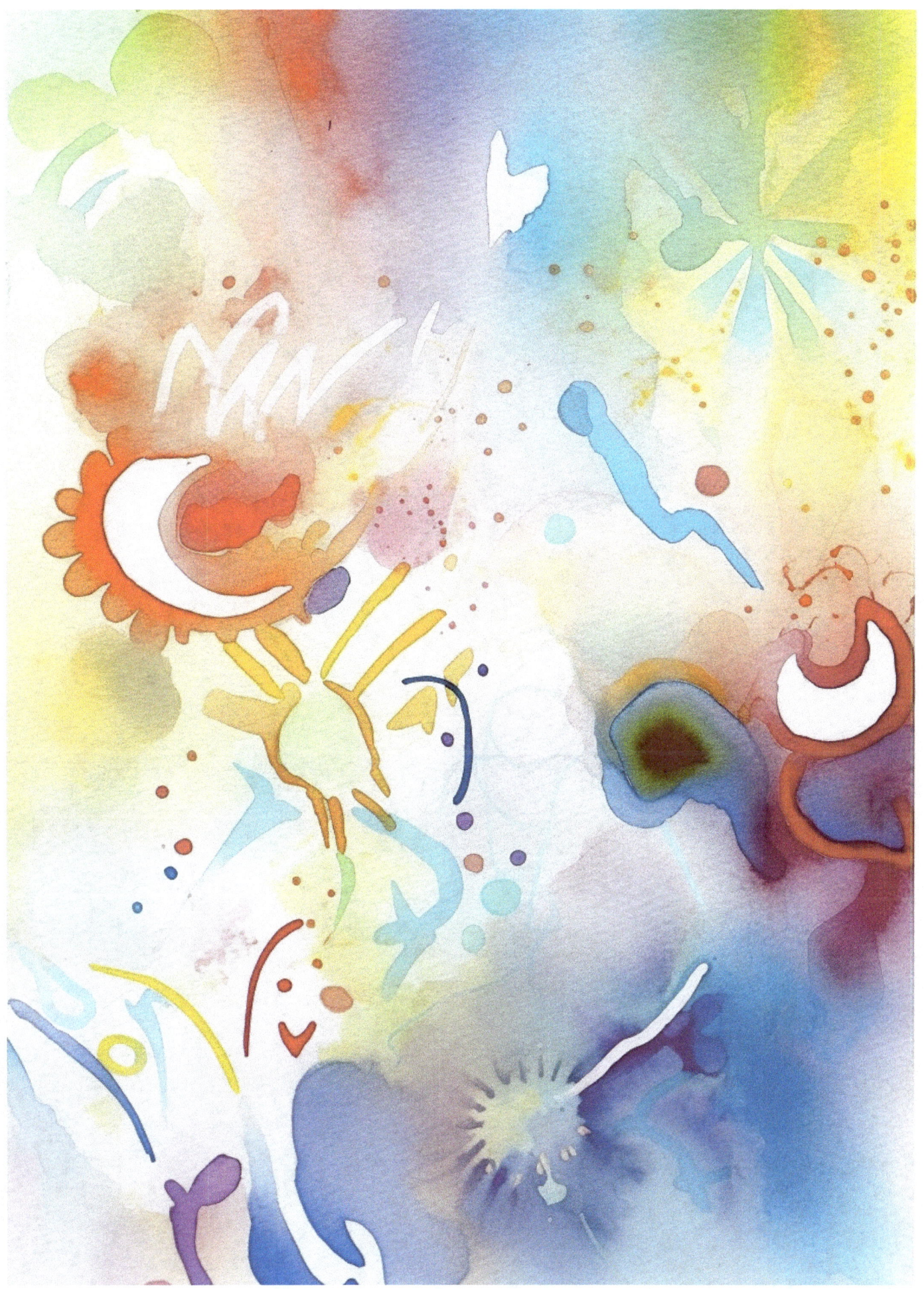

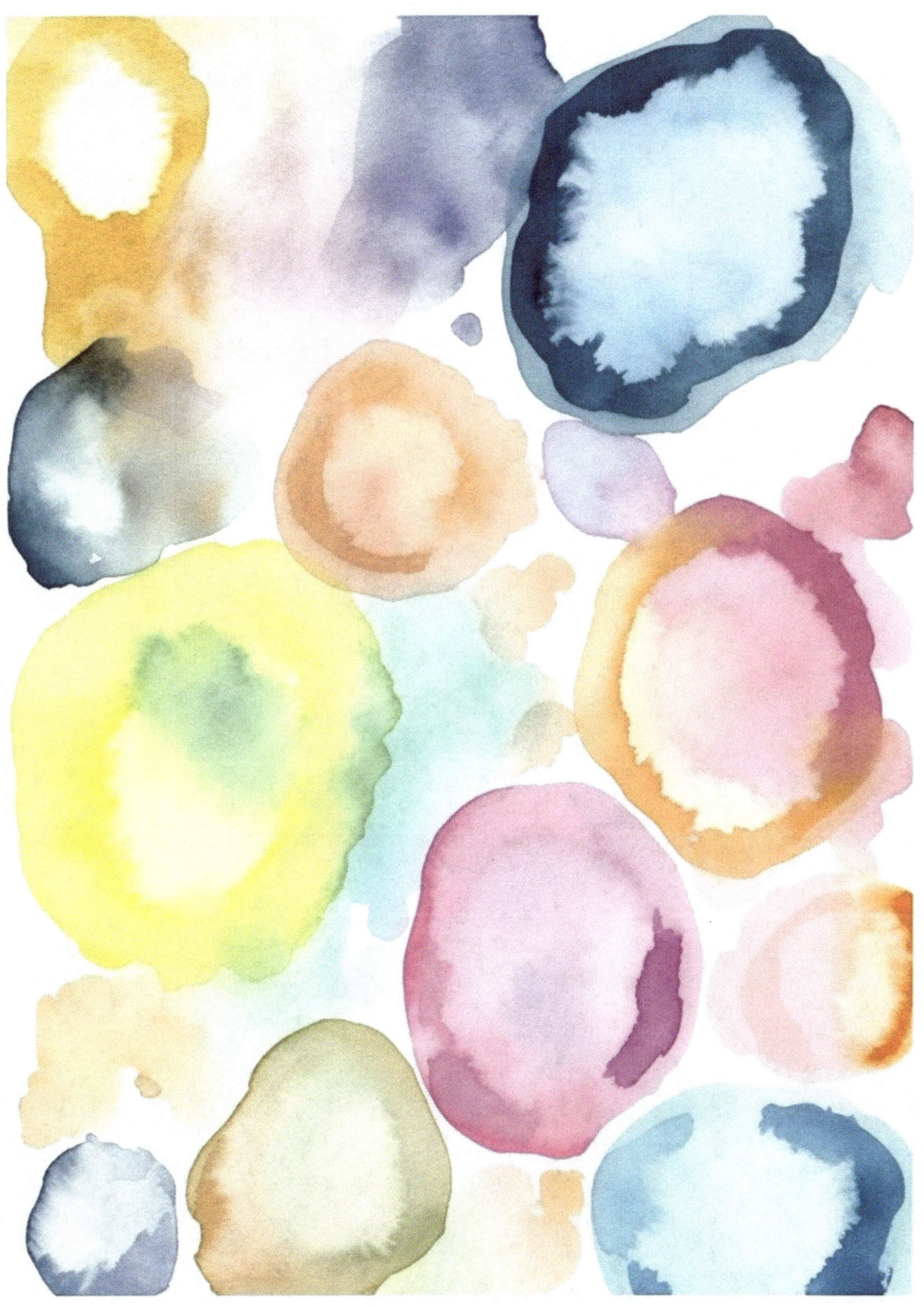

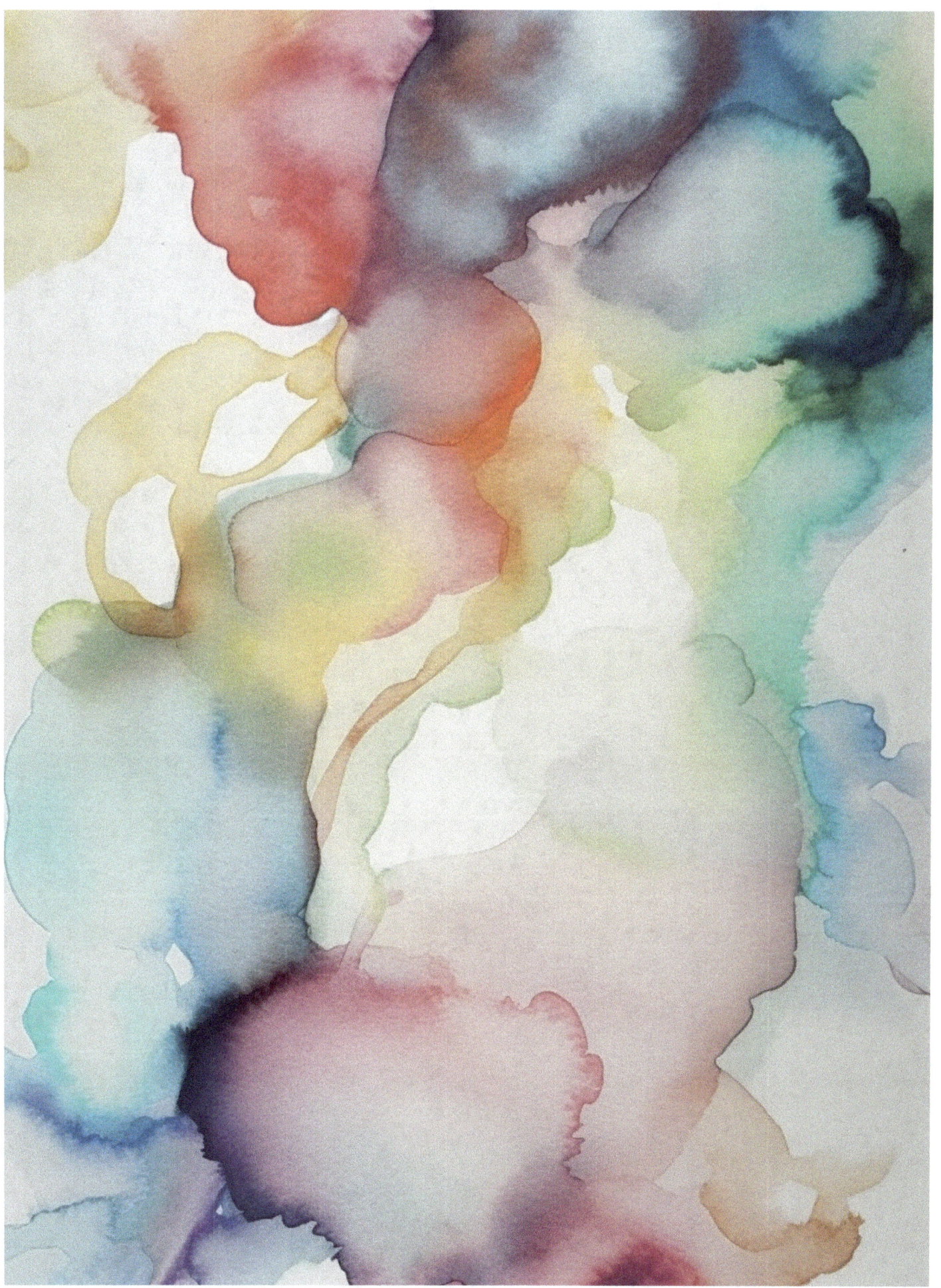

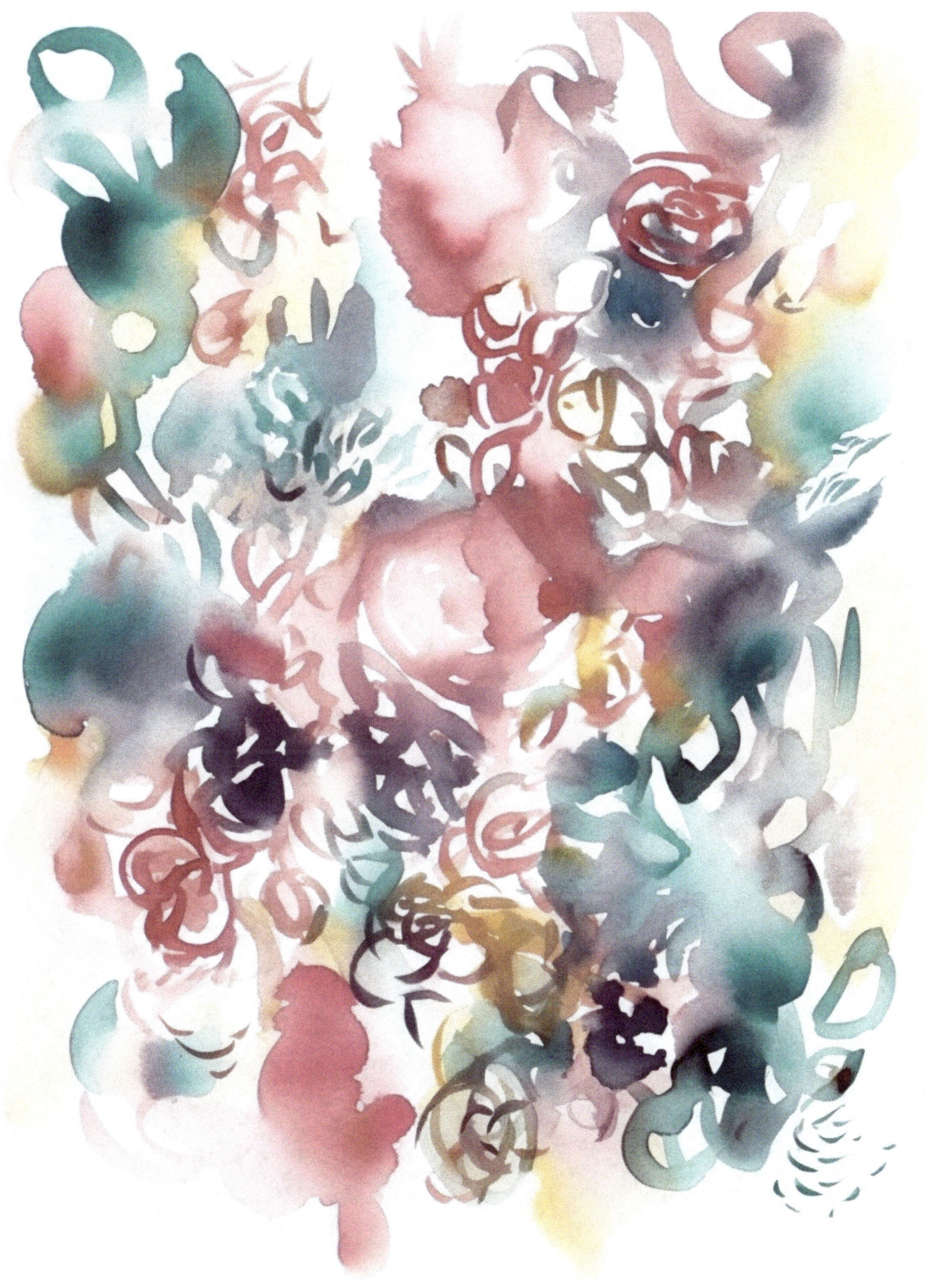

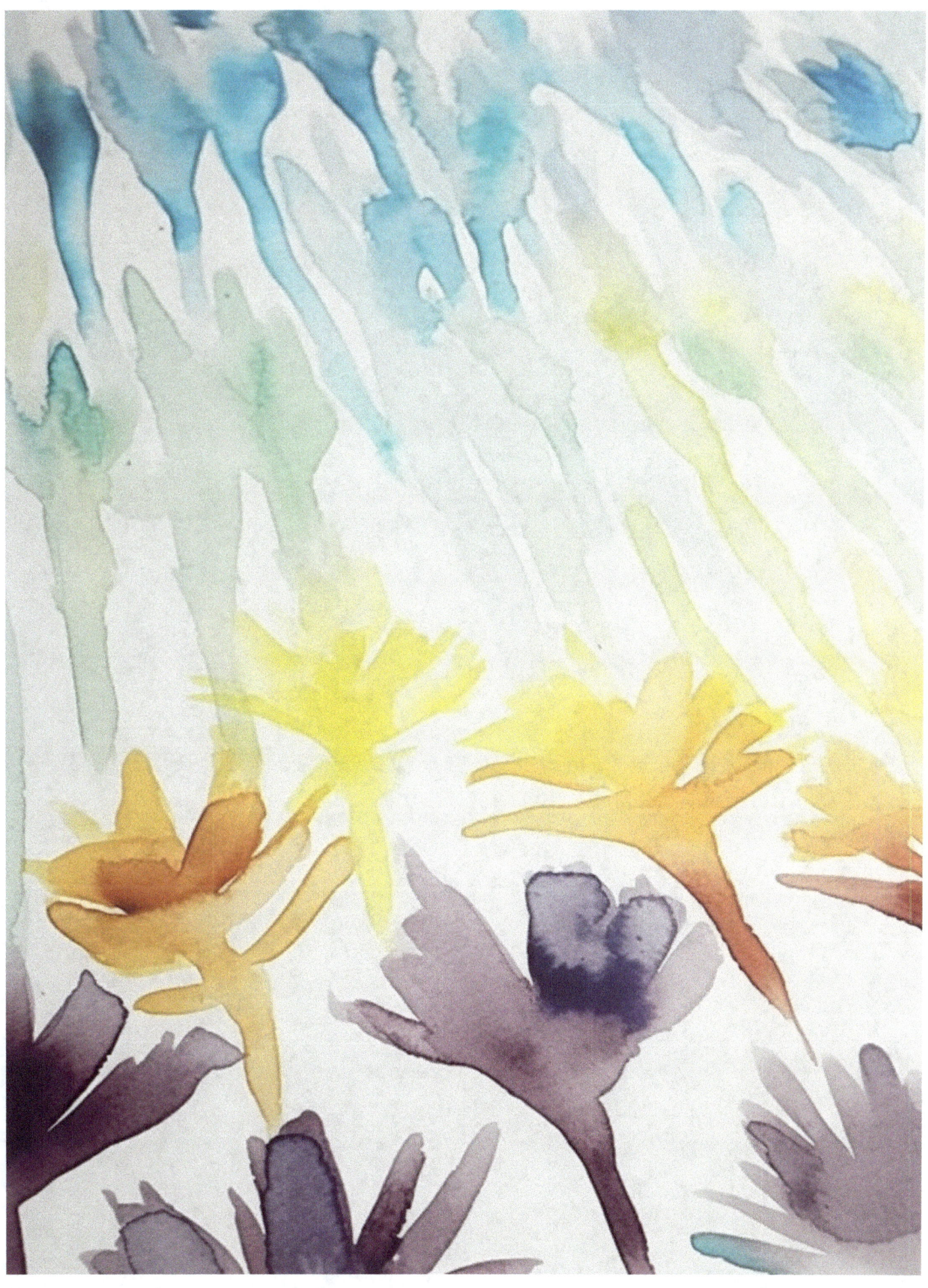

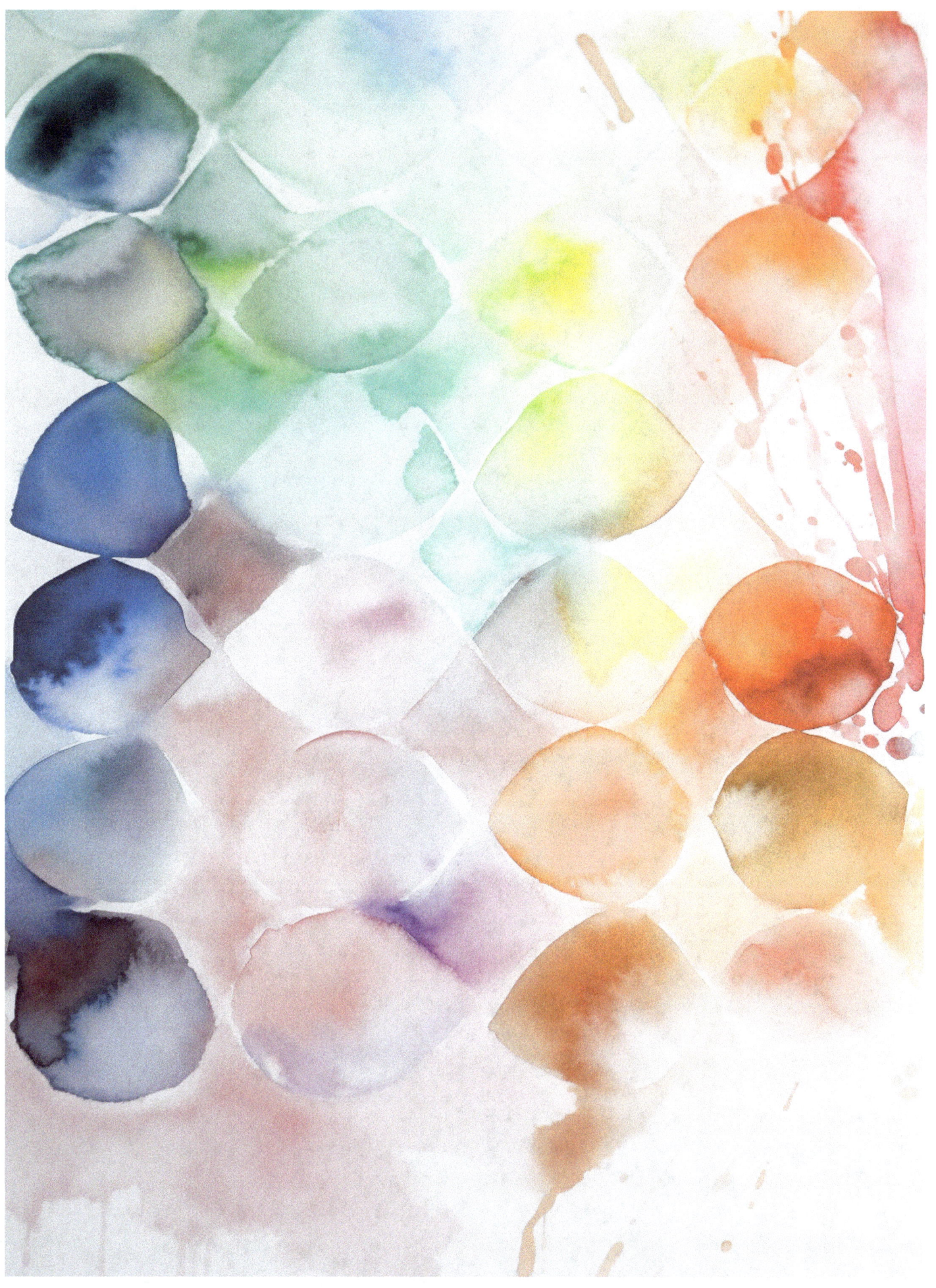

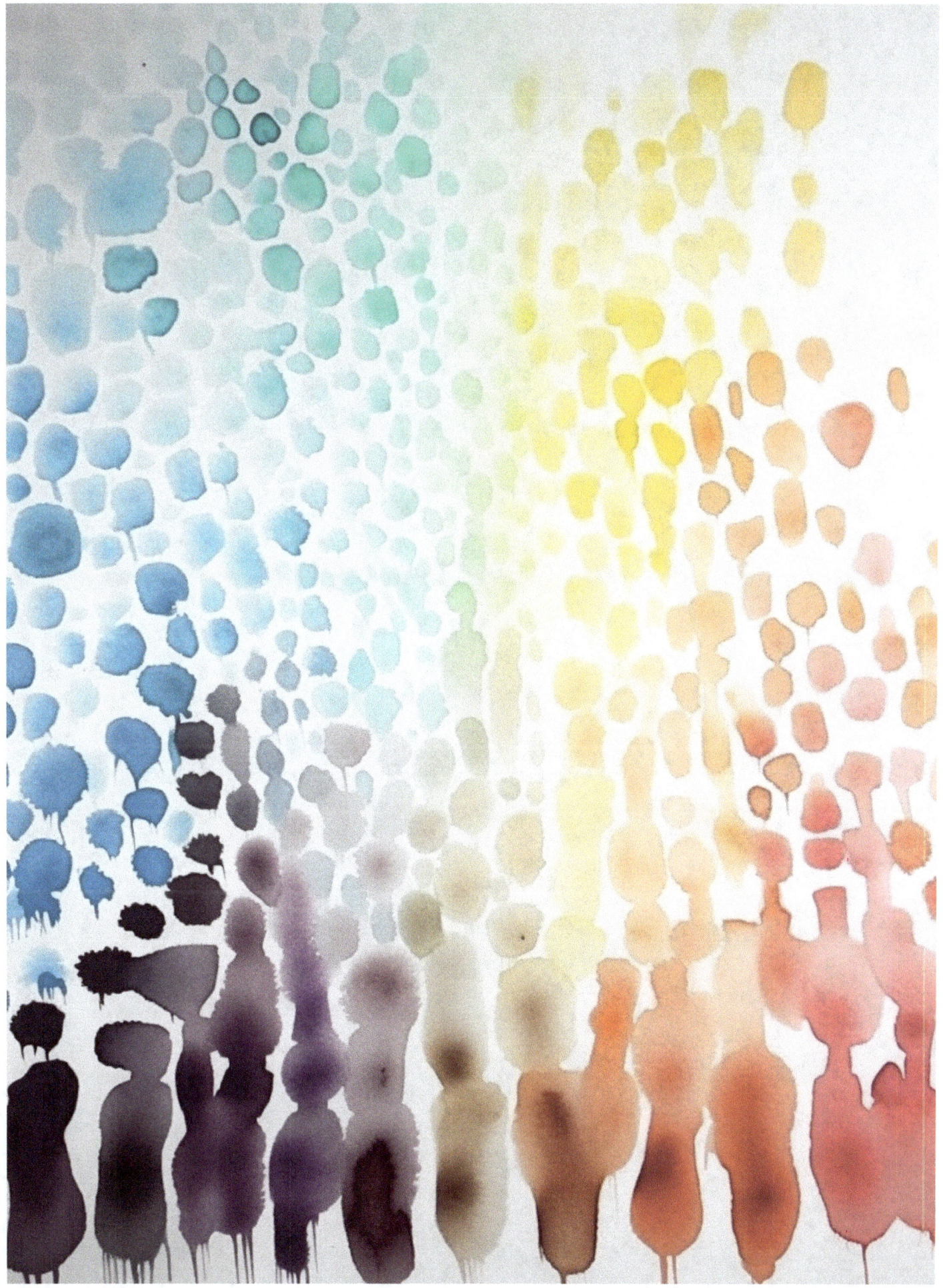

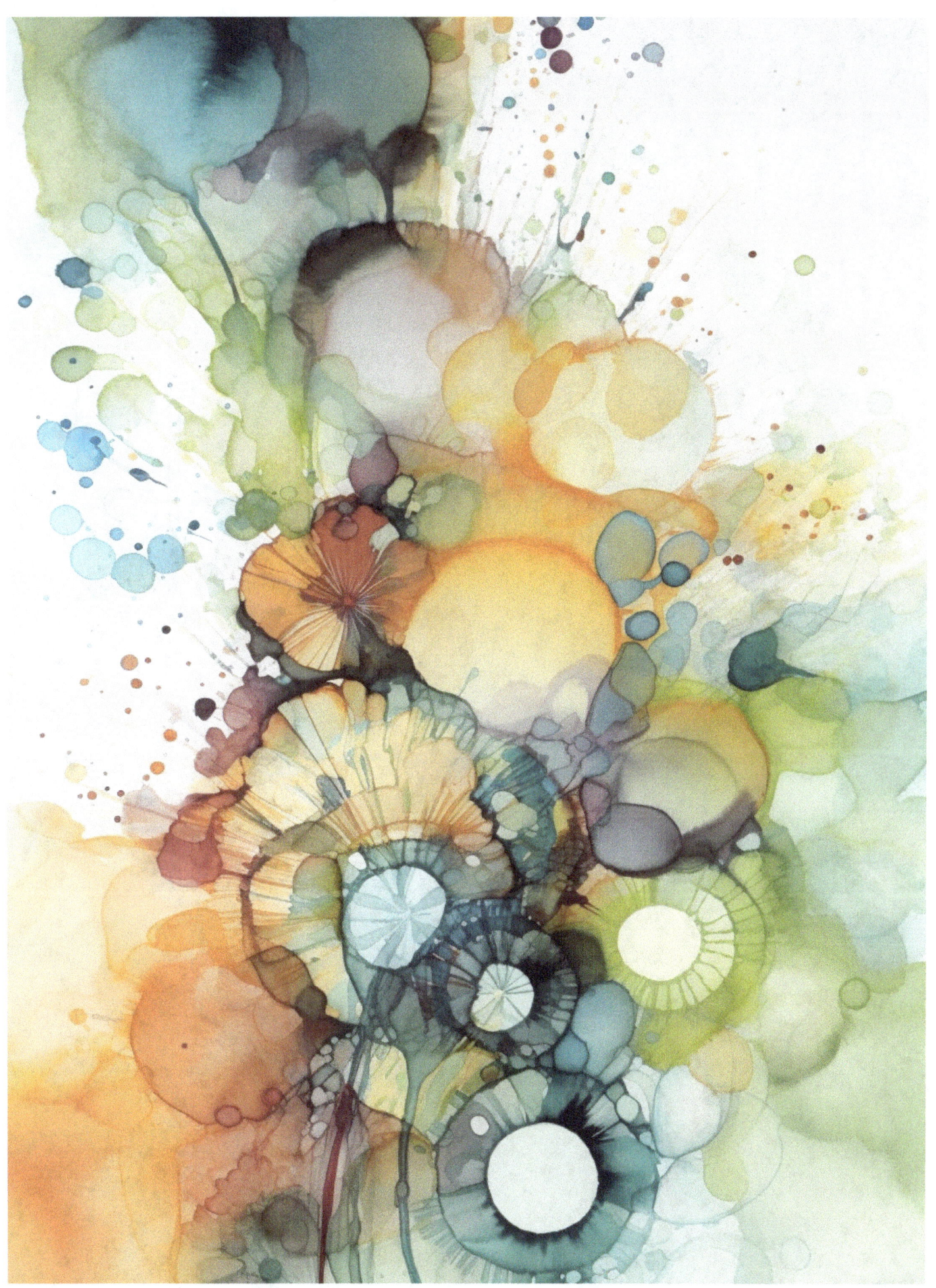

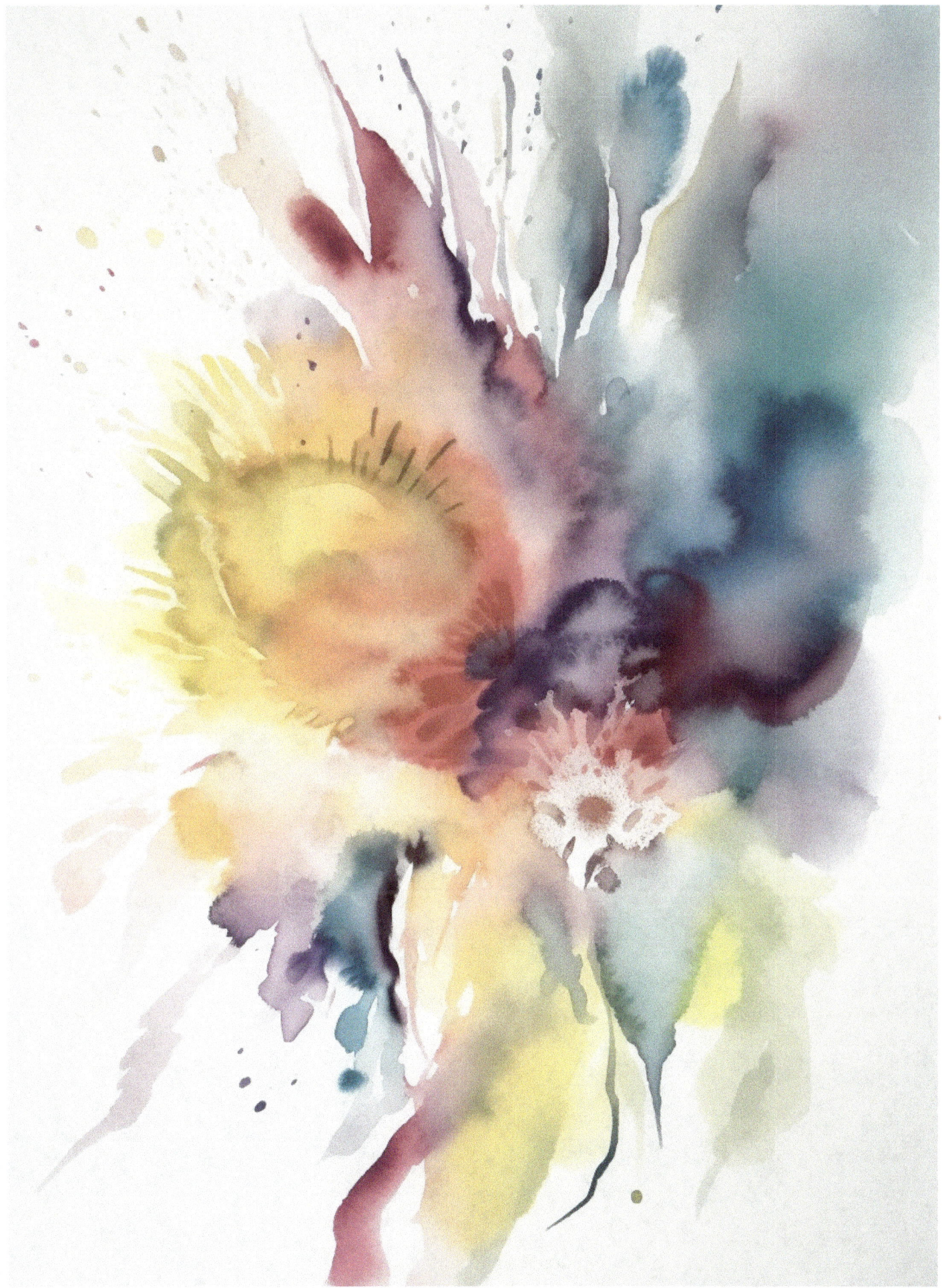

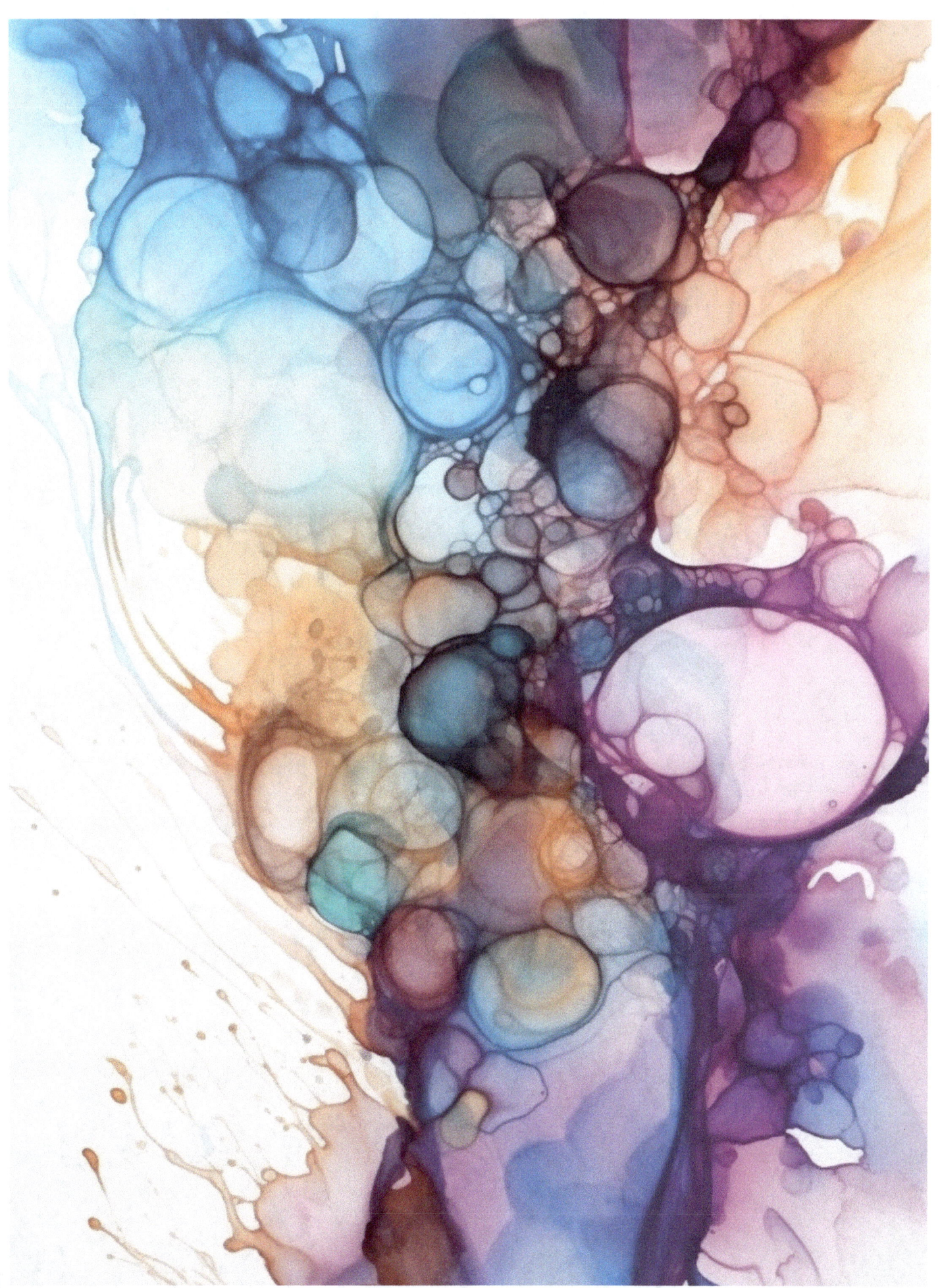

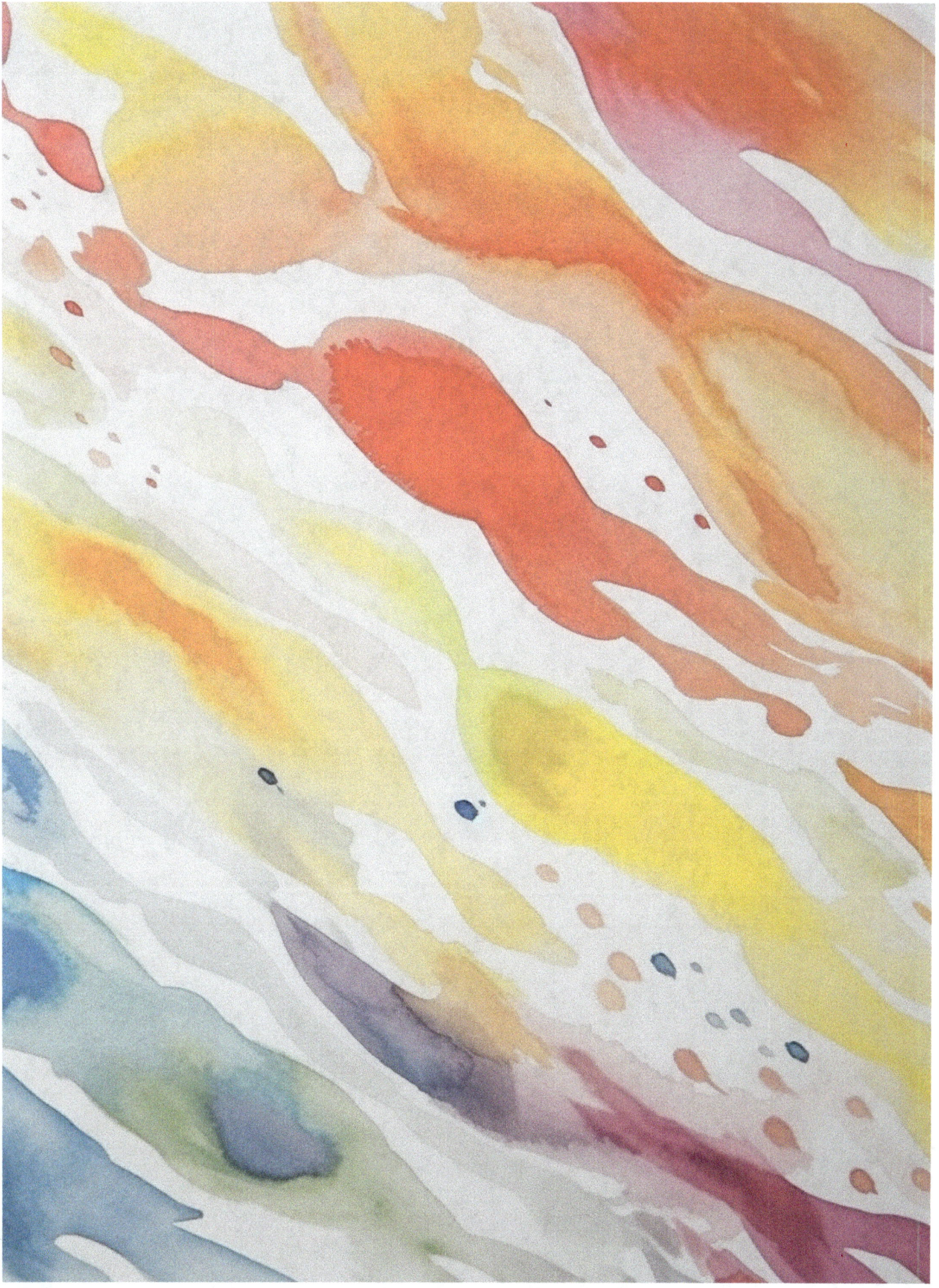

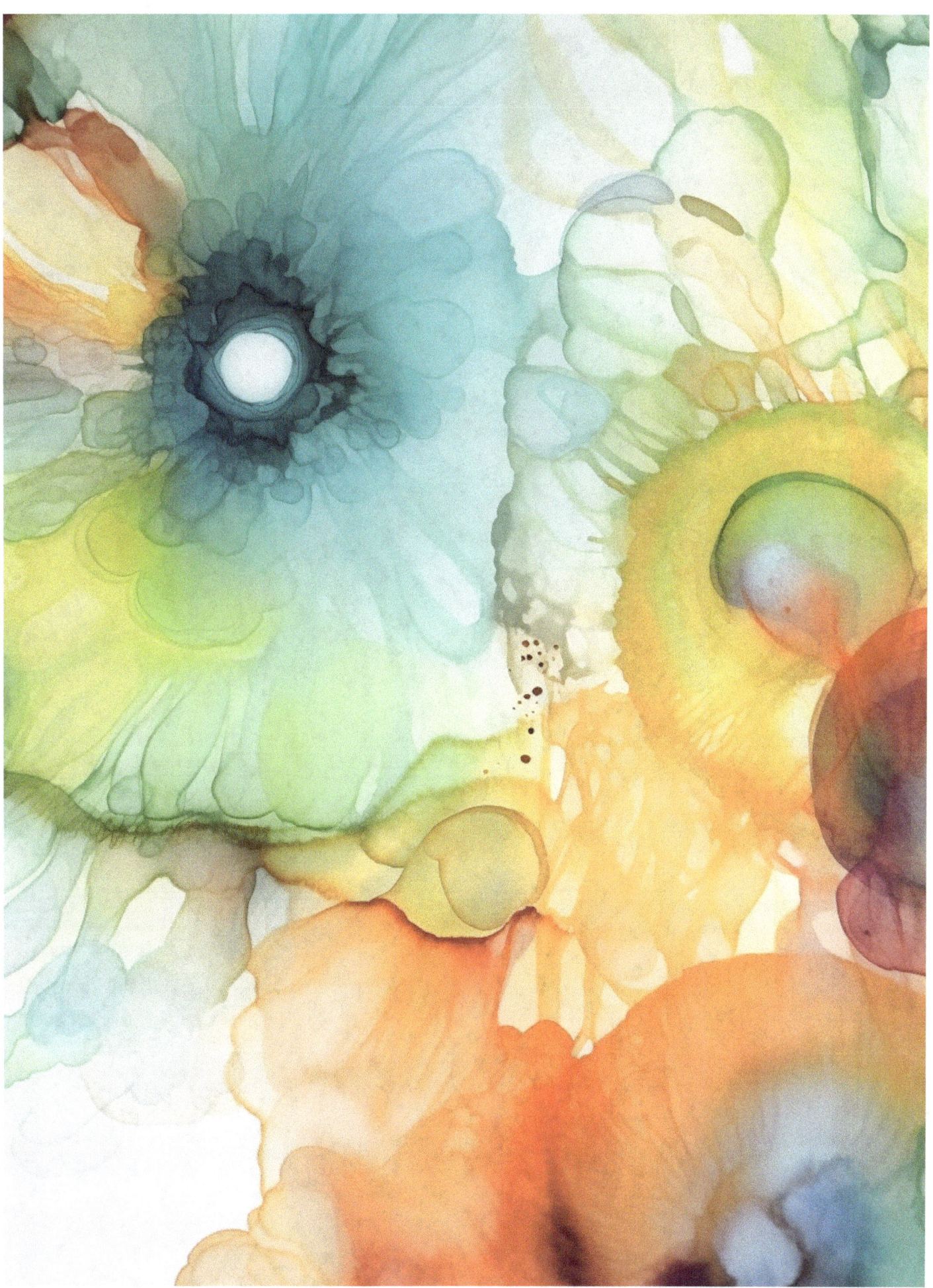

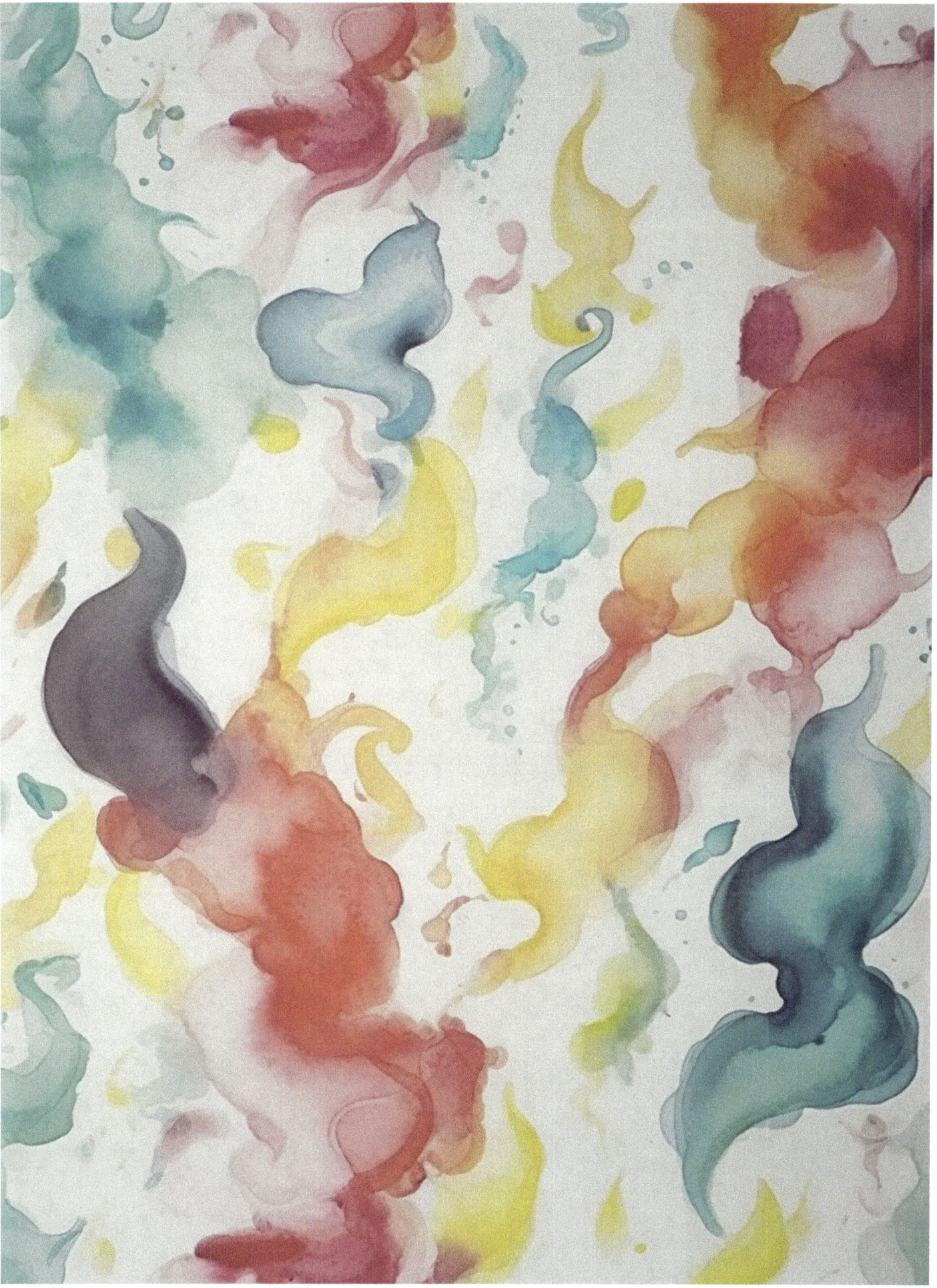

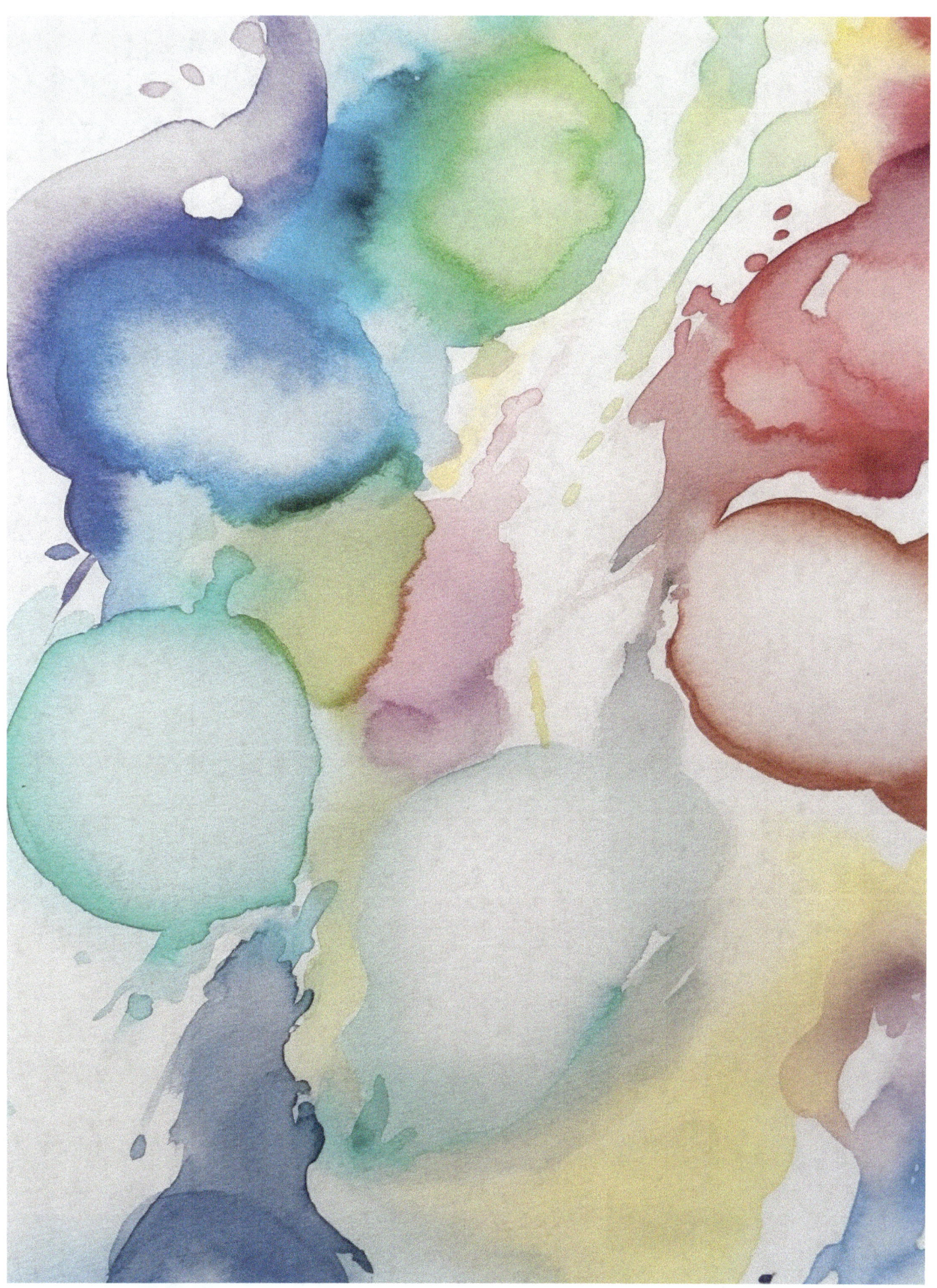

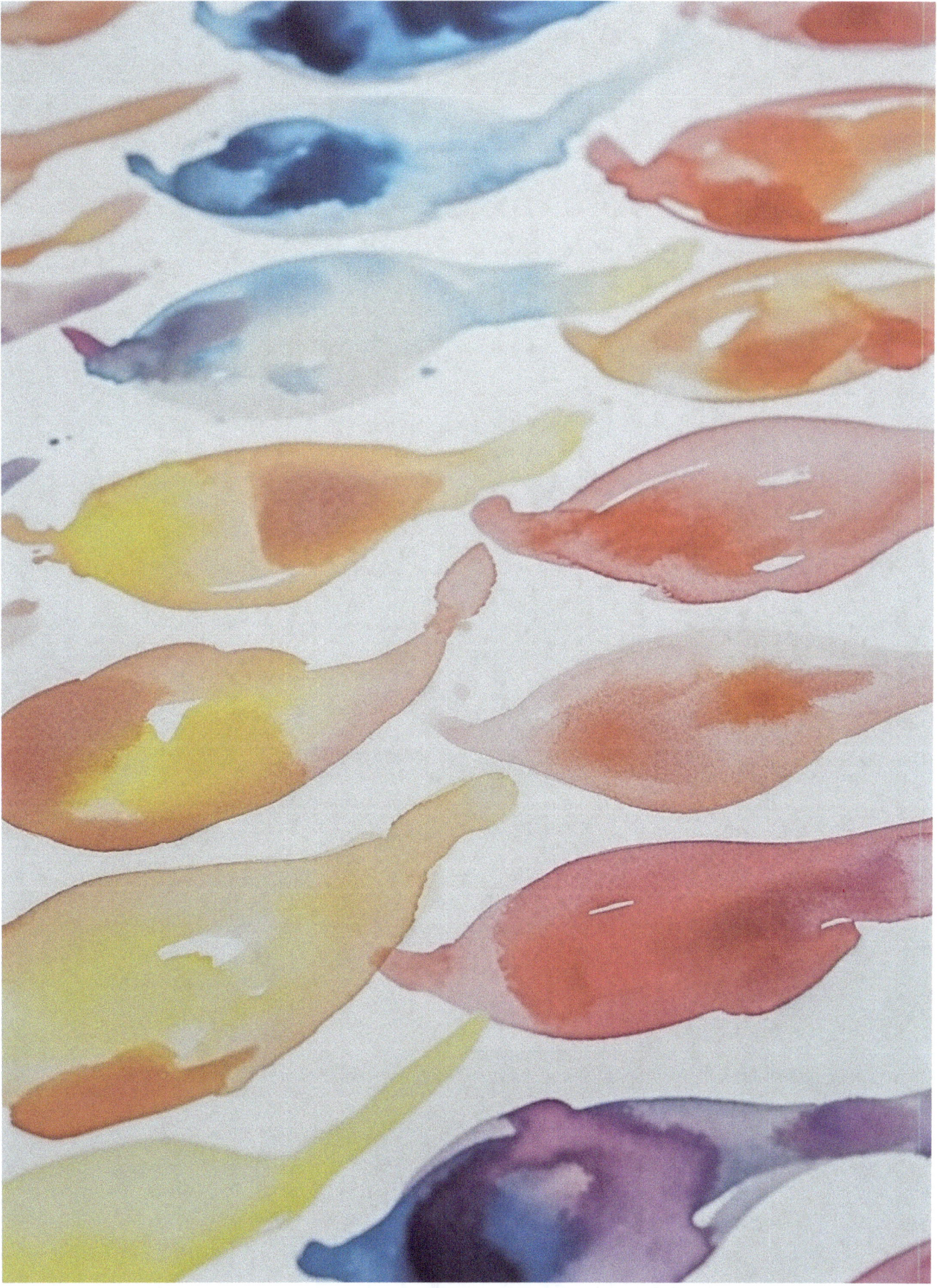

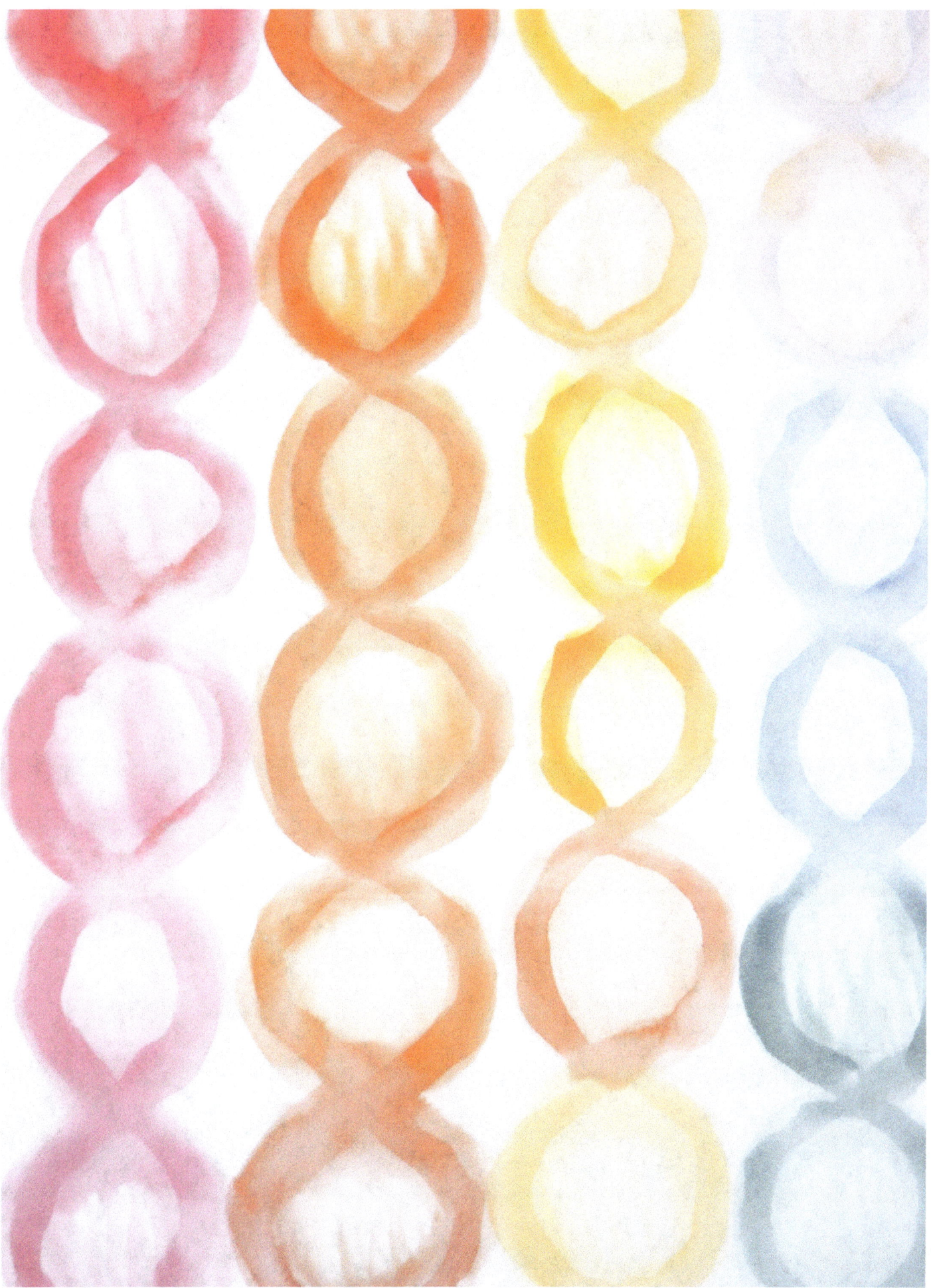

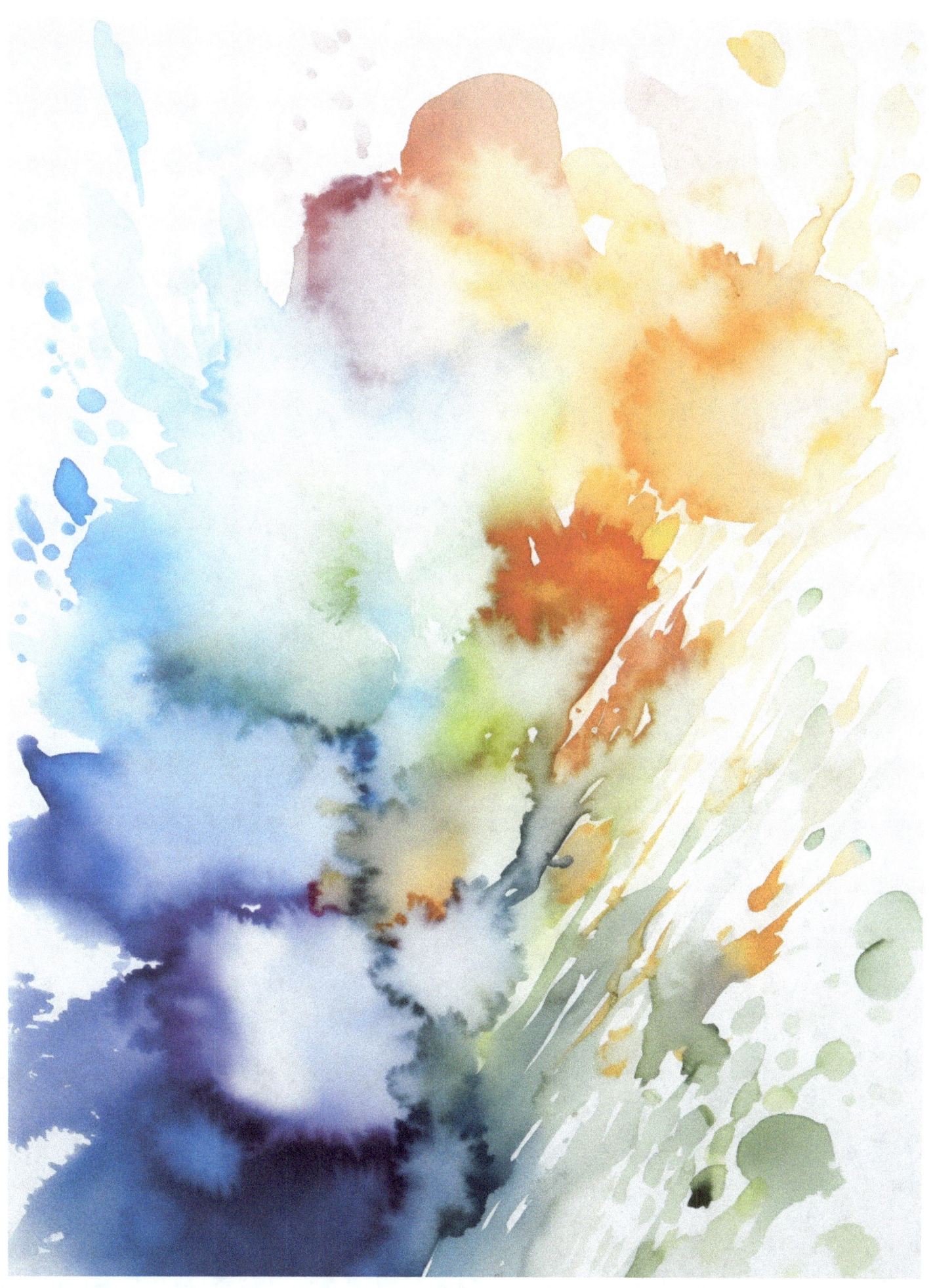

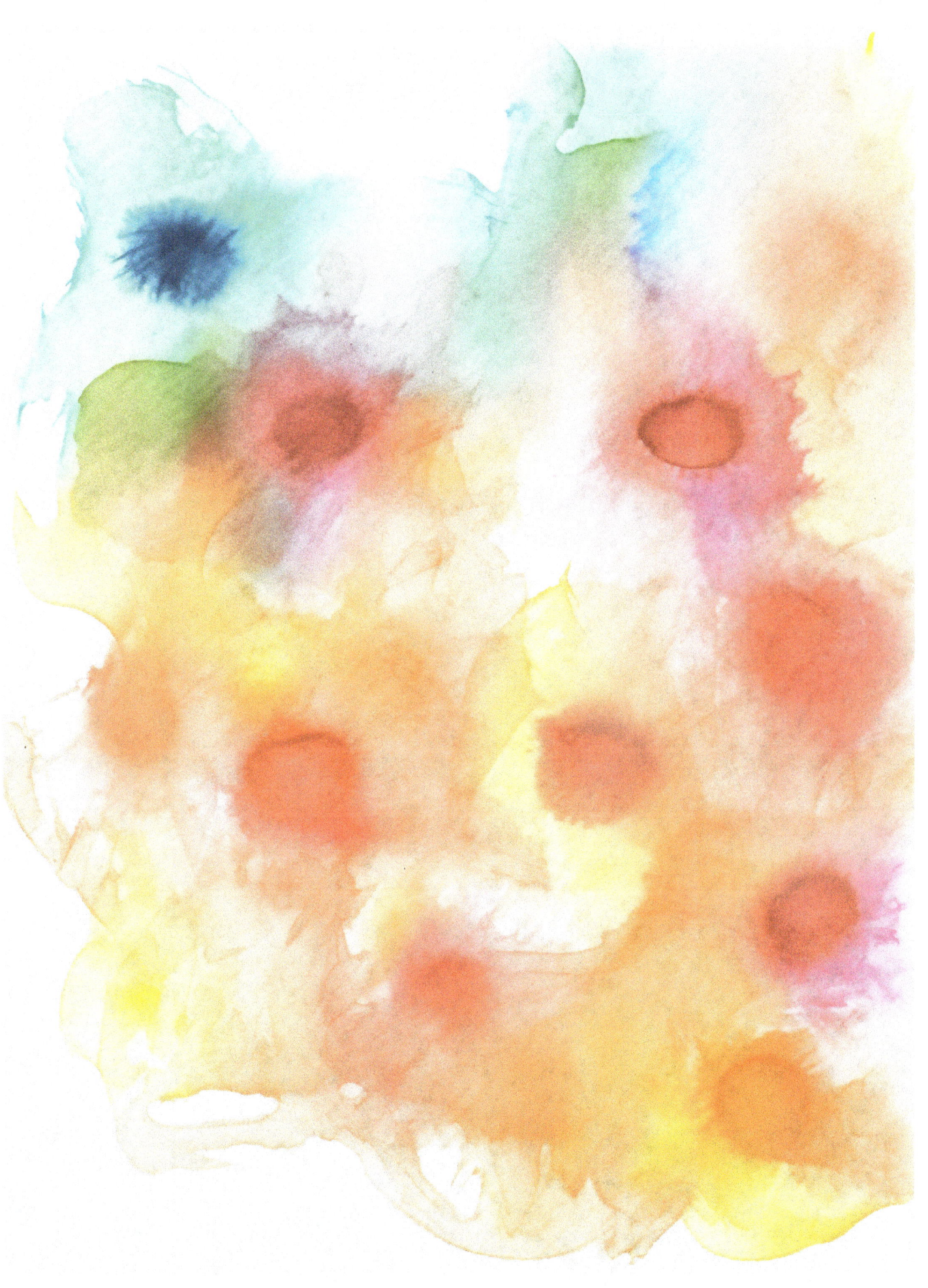

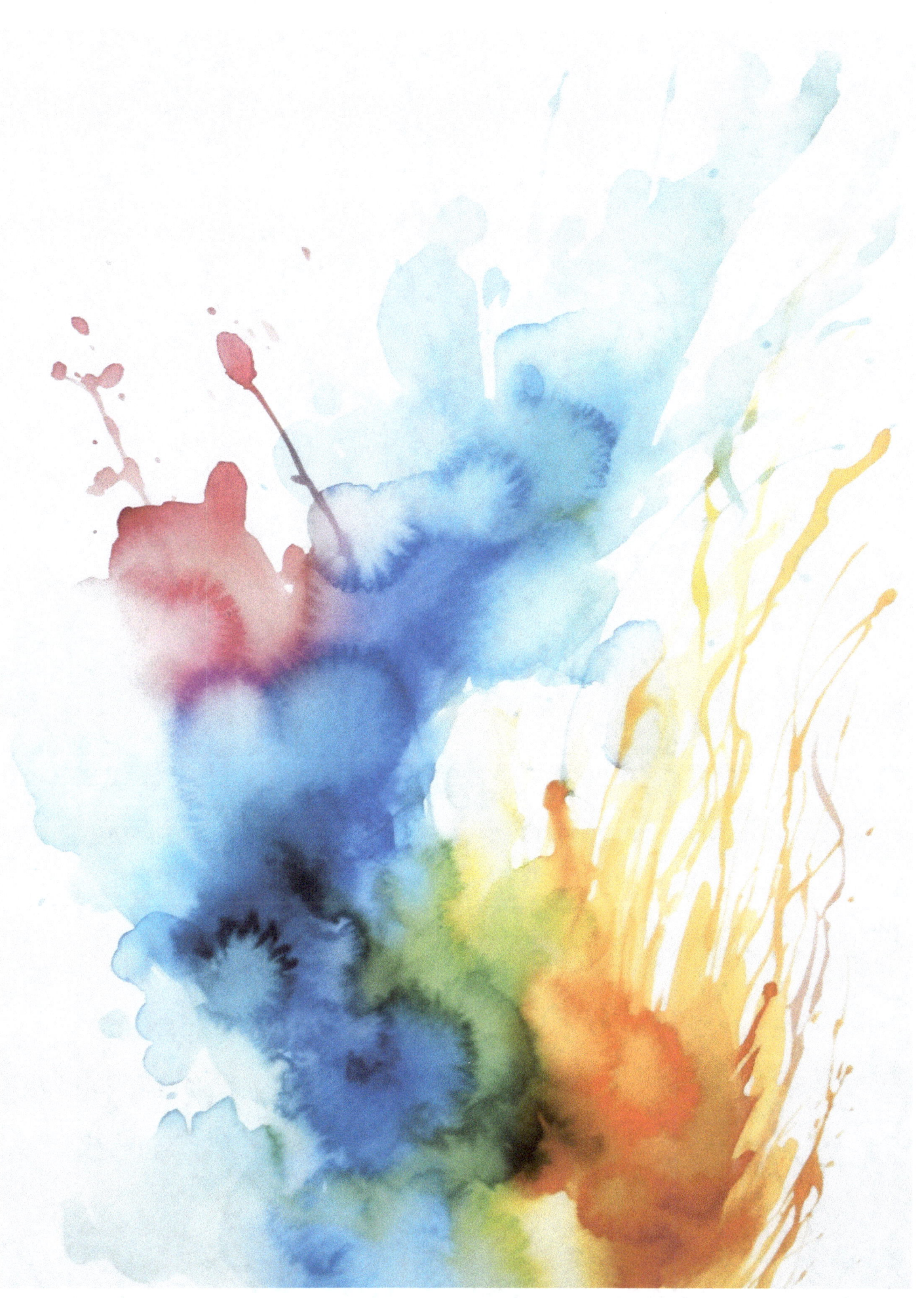

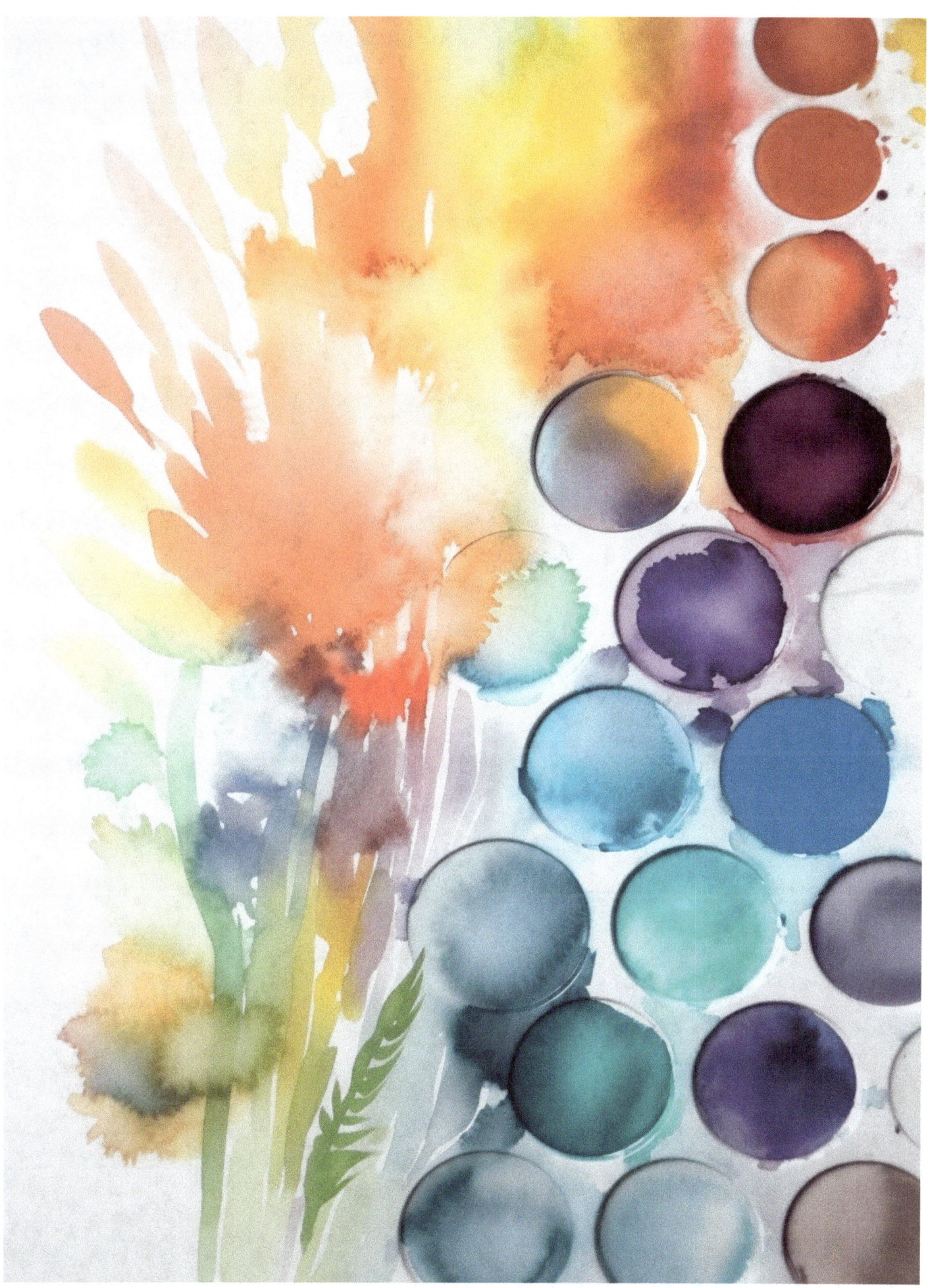

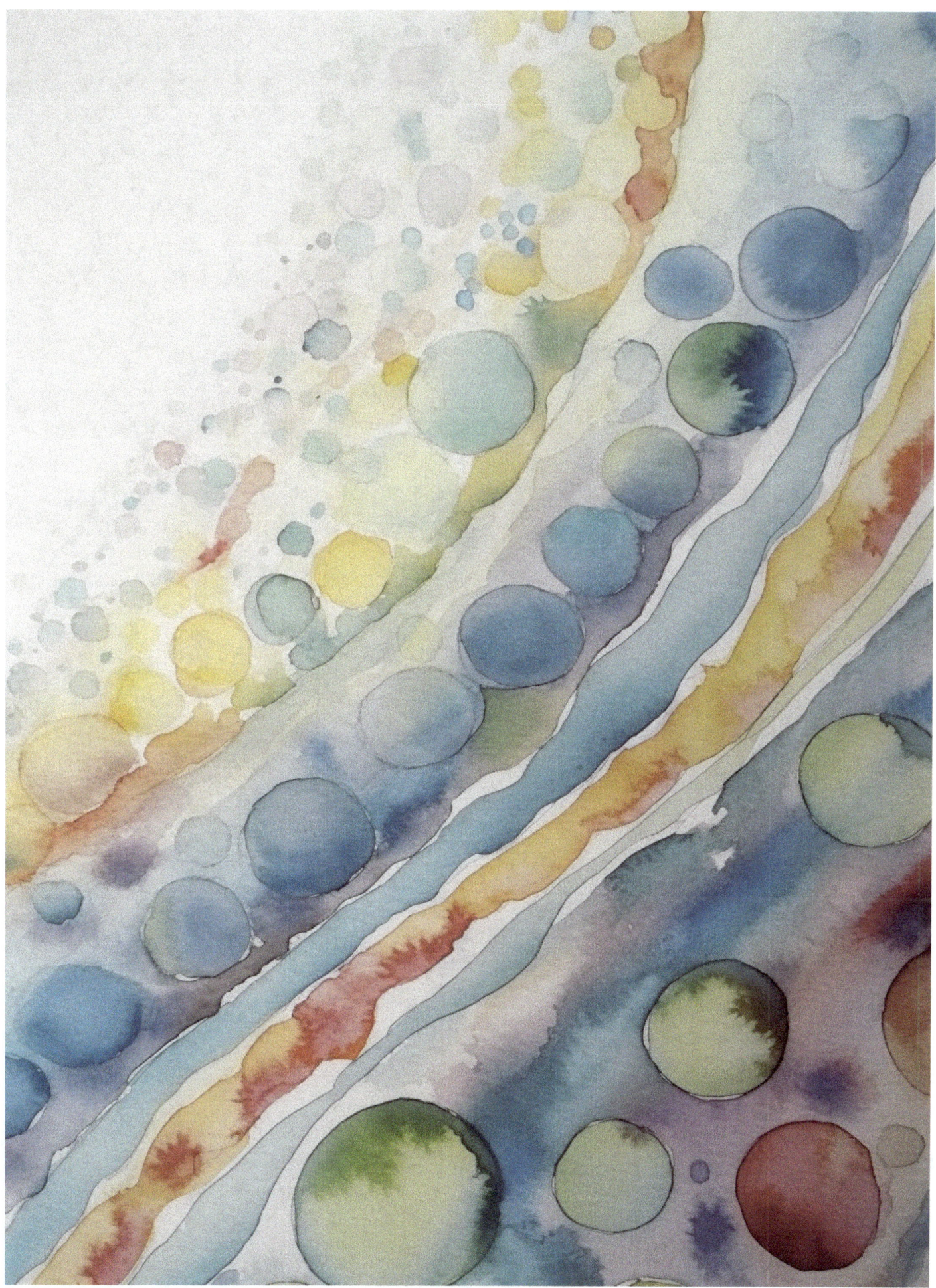

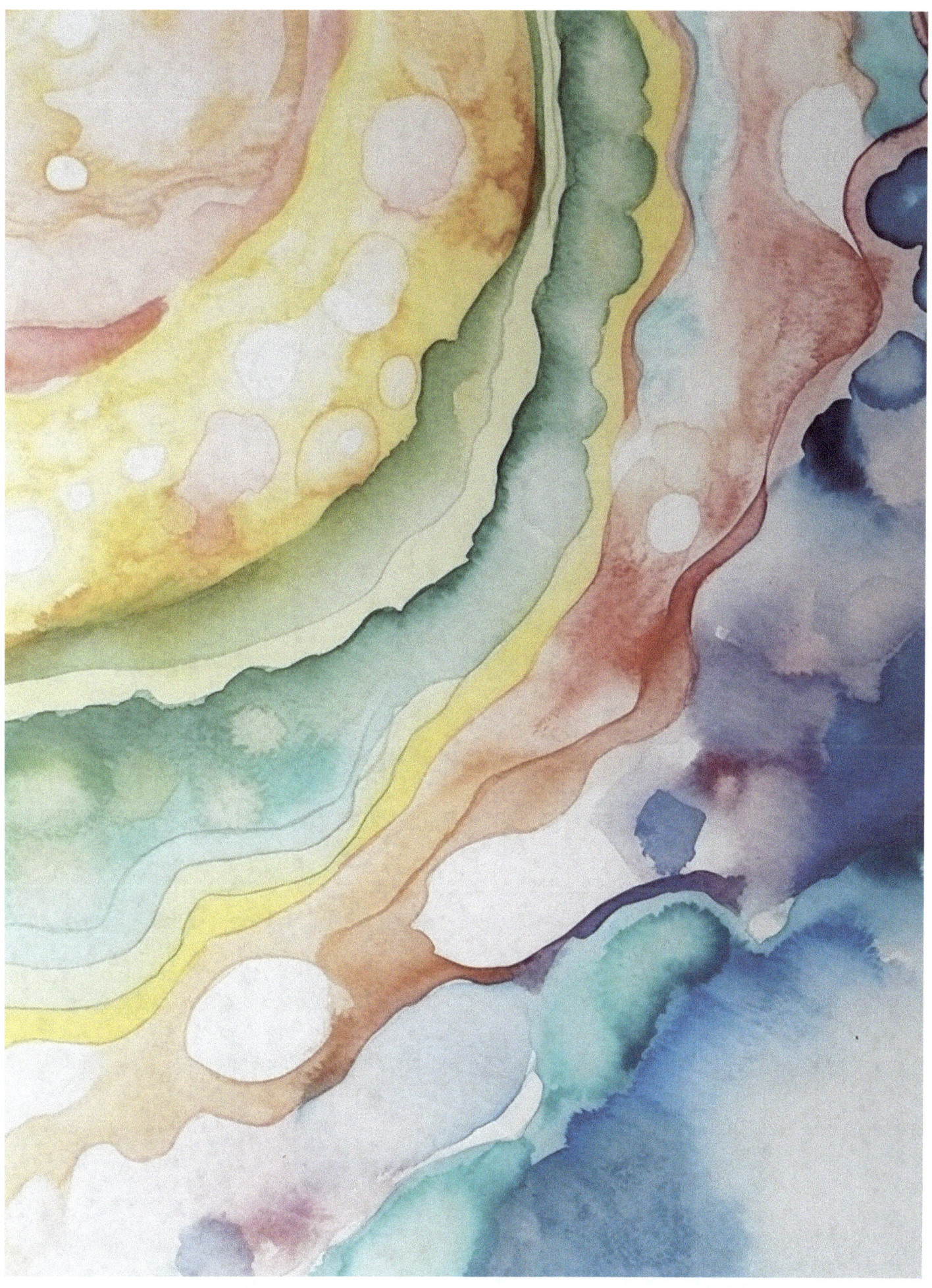

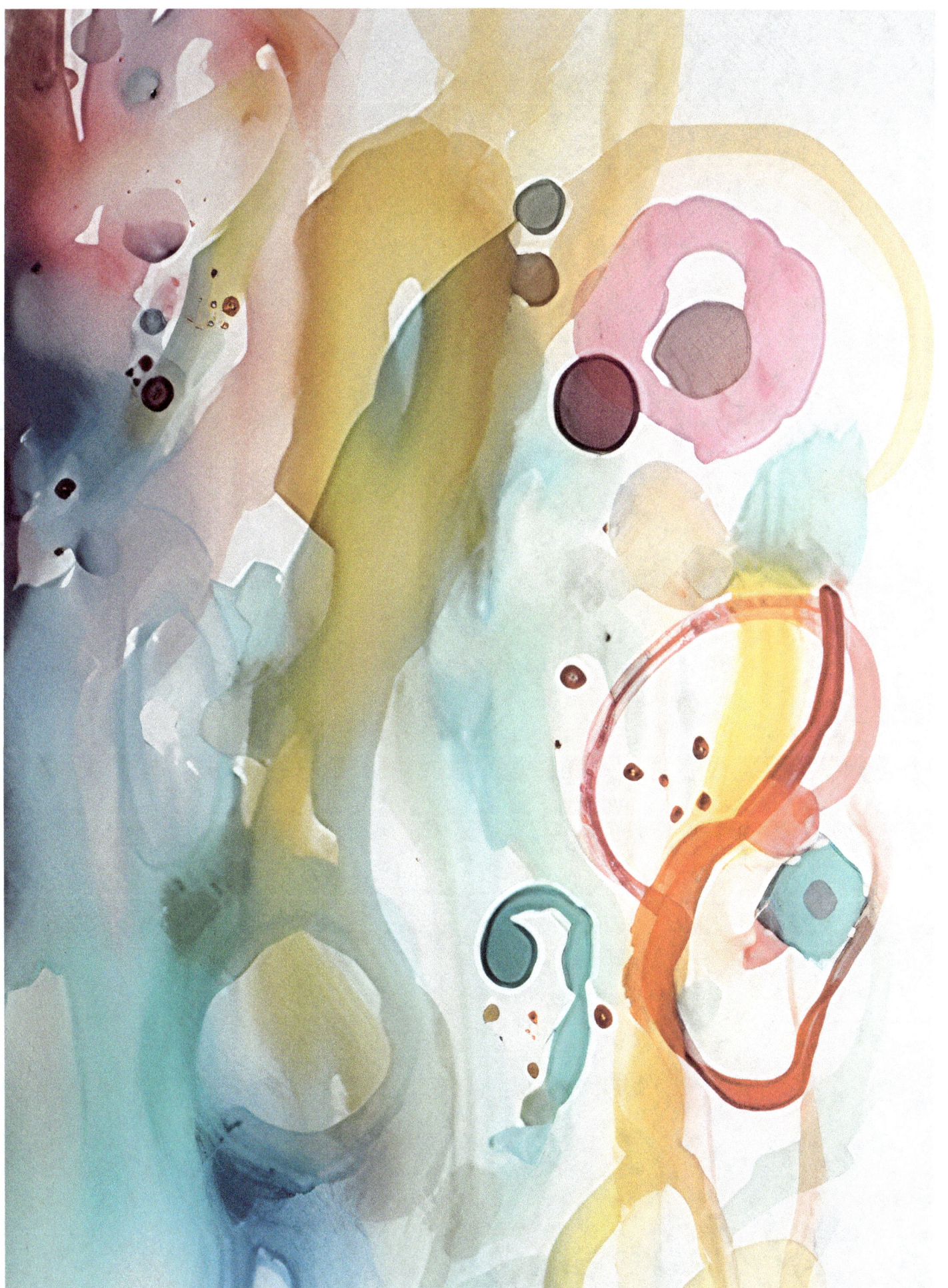

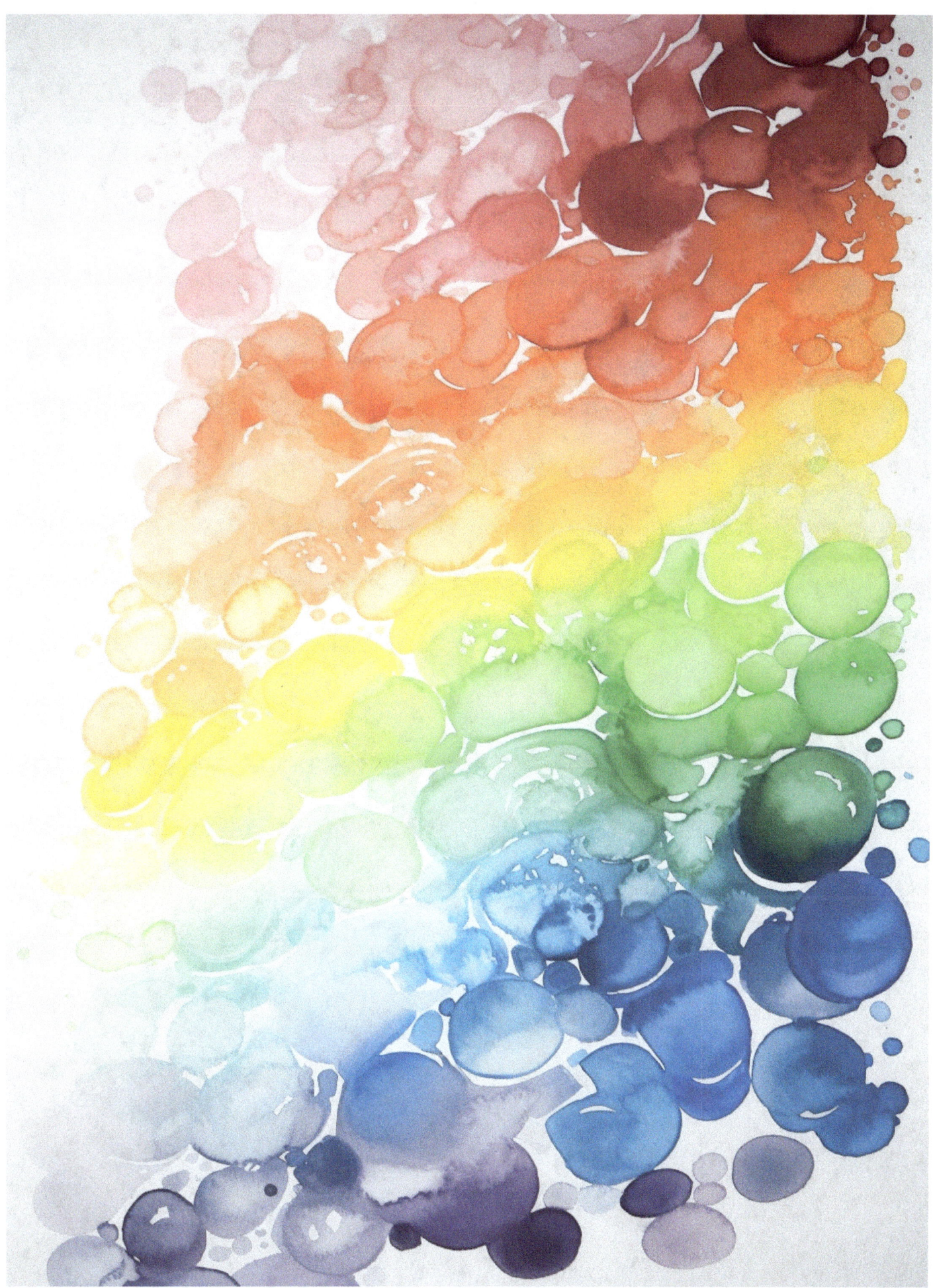

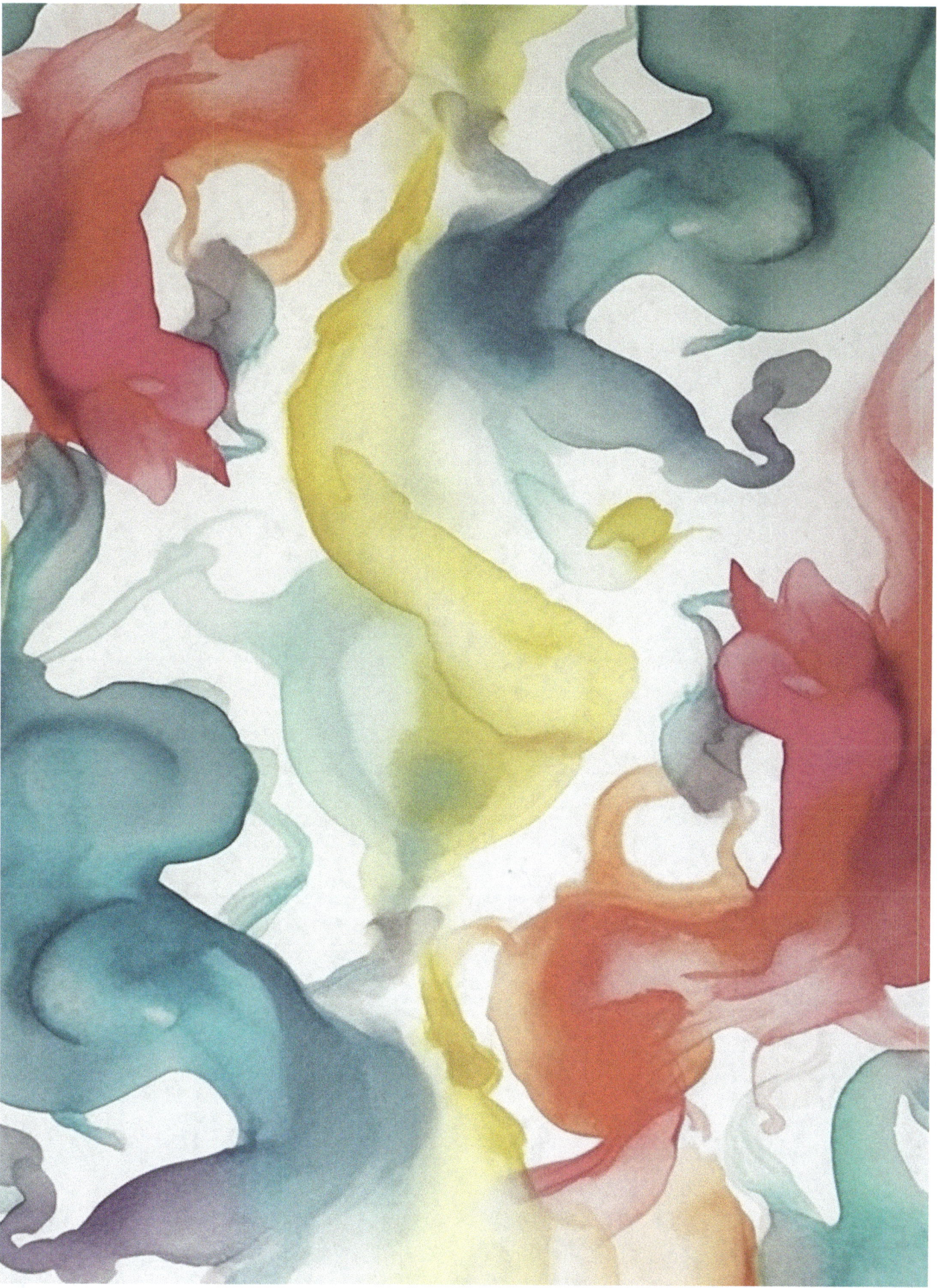

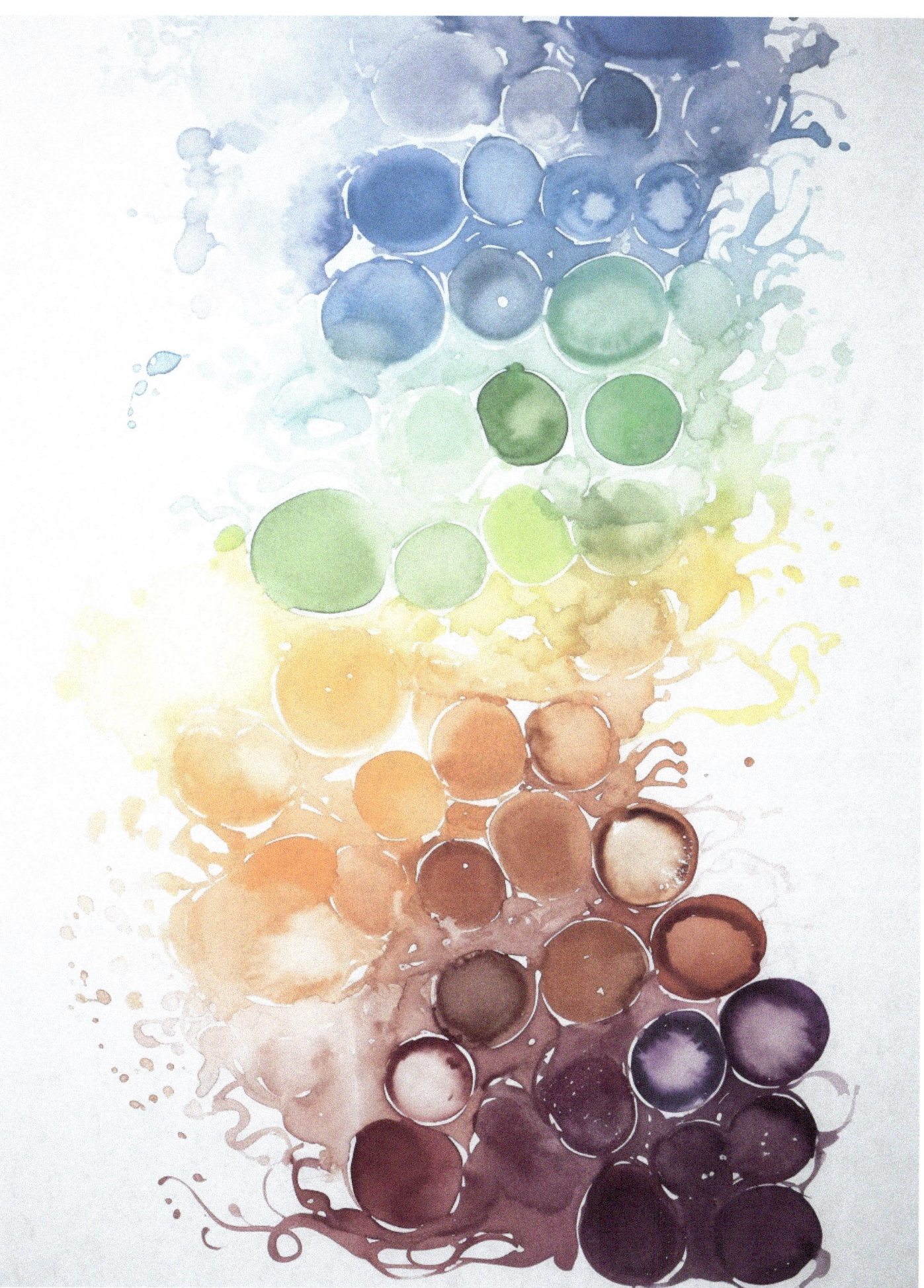

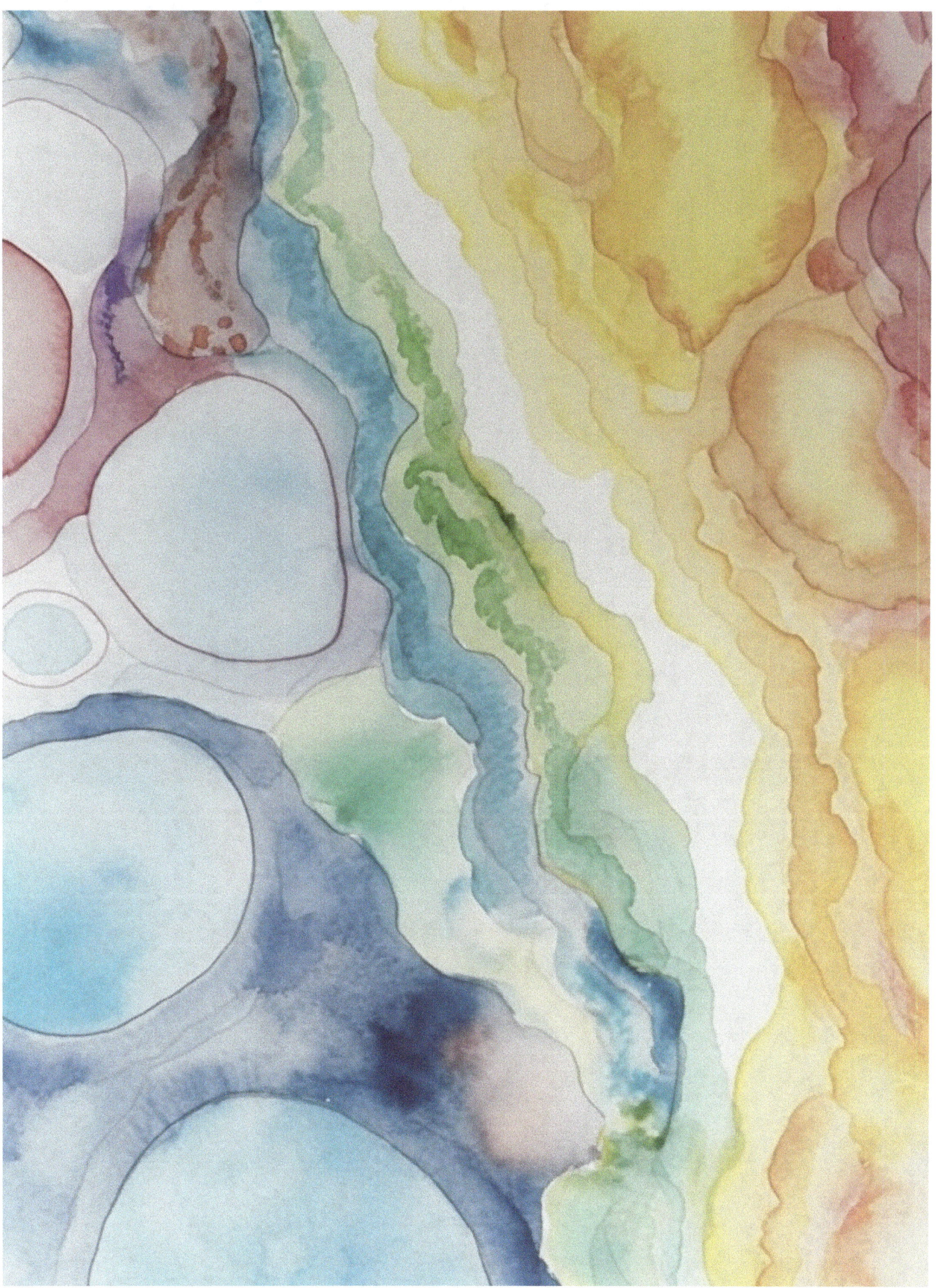

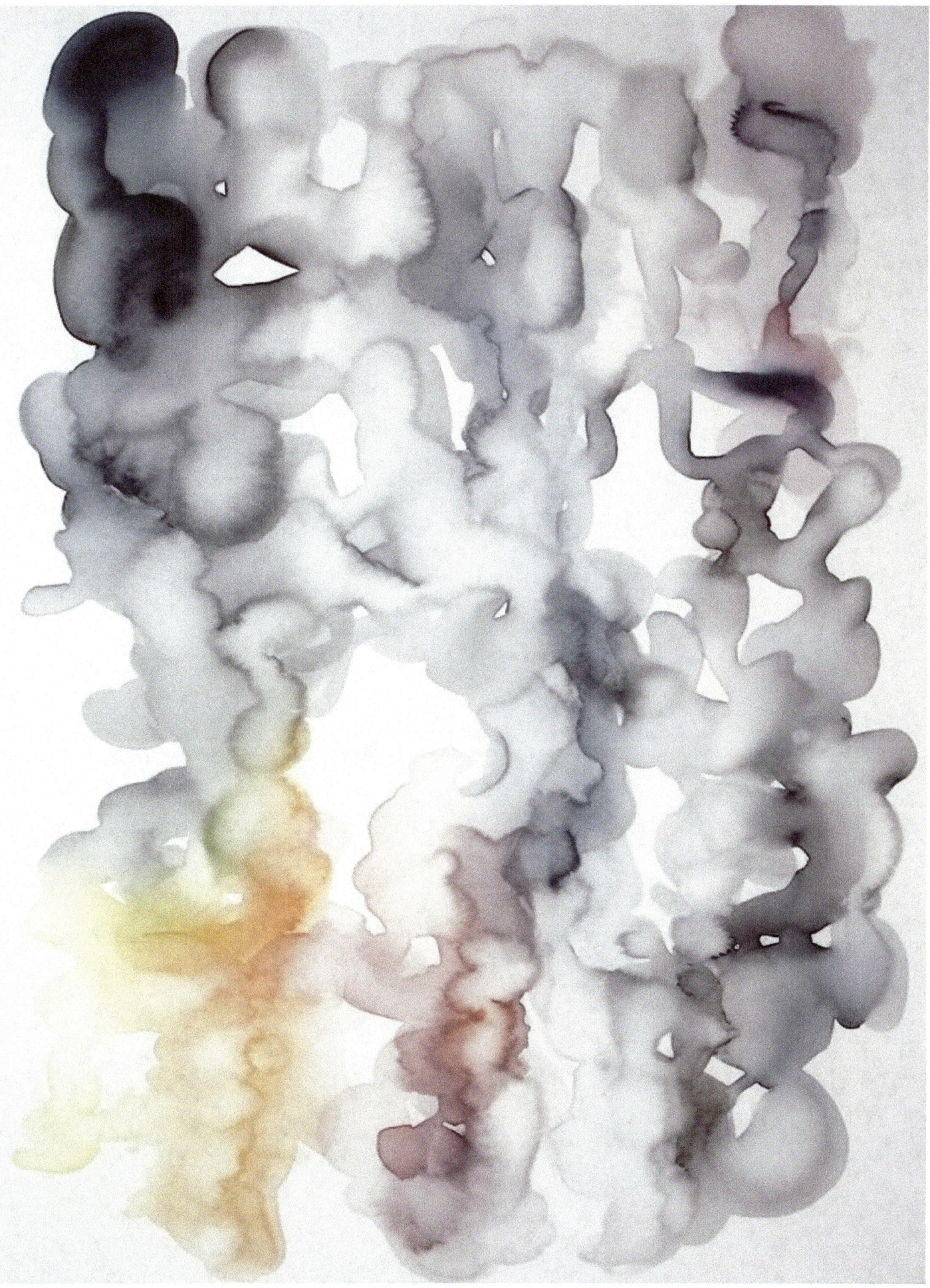

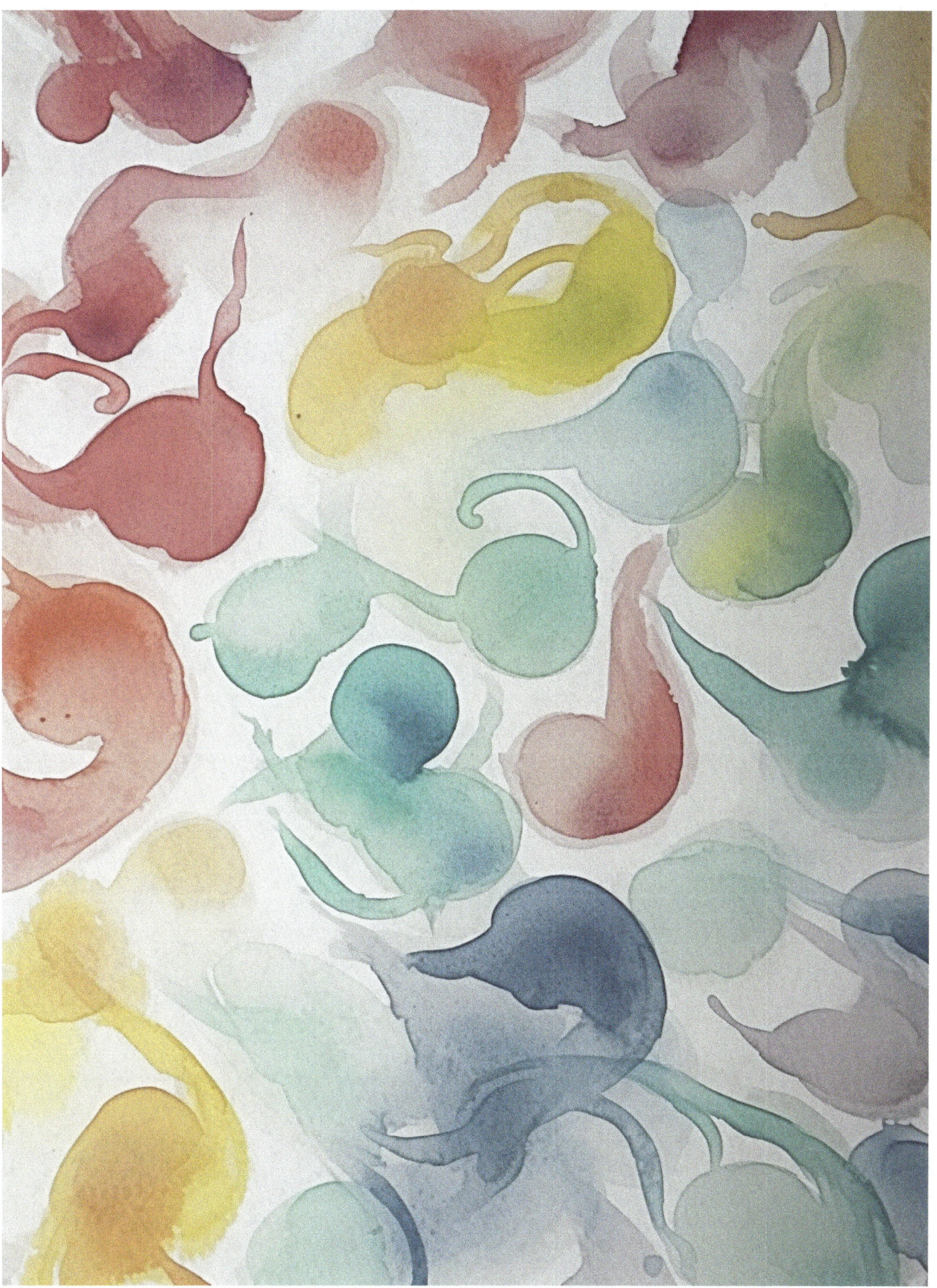

www.ingramcontent.com/pod-product-compliance
Lightning Source LLC
Chambersburg PA
CBHW082219290526
45794CB00009B/3600